# Living Science

PRINCETON ■ LONDON

Published in the United States and Canada by
Two-Can Publishing LLC
234 Nassau Street
Princeton, NJ 08542

www.two-canpublishing.com

Copyright © Two-Can Publishing, 2001
Series concept and original design: Wendy Baker and Andrew Haslam
Design copyright © Wendy Baker and Andrew Haslam
Design of models © 1994 Andrew Haslam
Cover designed by Picthall and Gunzi Ltd

'Two-Can' is a trademark of Two-Can Publishing
Two-Can Publishing is a division of Zenith Entertainment plc, 43–45 Dorset Street, London W1H 4AB

SC ISBN 1-58728-286-0
Hardback ISBN 1-58728-3786
2 3 4 5 6 7 8 9 10 02

MACHINES
Author: David Glover BSc PhD; Editor: Mike Hirst; Photography: Jon Barnes; Series Consultant: John Chaldecott;
Science Consultant: Graham Peacock, Lecturer in Science Education, Sheffield Hallam University, UK; Additional design: Helen McDonagh;
Thanks also to: Rachel and Catherine Bee, Elizabeth Bricknell, and everyone at Plough Studios

ELECTRICITY
Author: Alexandra Parsons; Editor: Mike Hirst; Illustrators: Diana Leadbetter and Michael Ogden;
Photography: Jon Barnes; Series Consultant: John Chaldecott; Science Consultant: Graham Peacock, Lecturer in Science Education,
Sheffield City Polytechnic Centre for Science Education, UK; Additional photography: John Englefield;
Additional editorial and design work: Sharon Nowakowski, Carole Orbell, Robert Sved and Belinda Webster.

SOUND
Author: Alexandra Parsons; Editor: Mike Hirst; Illustrator: Michael Ogden; Photography: Jon Barnes;
Additional design: Belinda Webster; Thanks also to: Albert Baker, Catherine Bee, Tony Ellis, and everyone at Plough Studios

BUILDING
Author: David Glover BSc PhD; Editor: Kate Asser; Photography: Jon Barnes; Assistant model-maker: Sarah Davies;
Additional design: Lisa Nutt; Special thanks to: Karen Ingebretsen

Printed in Hong Kong

**Be Careful!** Electricity can be very dangerous. All the activities in this book use batteries as the power source.
You should **never** experiment with household electricity or the plugs and sockets in your home.

Words marked in **bold** are explained in the glossary

# Contents

# Machines

Humans are the only animals that invent and make machines. We use them to build skyscrapers, lift heavy loads, and move faster than the speed of sound. Humans have even made machines that can travel to the moon.

## MAKE it WORK!

You don't have to build robots or space rockets to be an engineer. In fact, engineers often make very simple machines. The projects in this book will show you how some machines are made, what they can do, and how they work. They'll also show you some engineering experiments. You might even be able to use the ideas for inventions of your own!

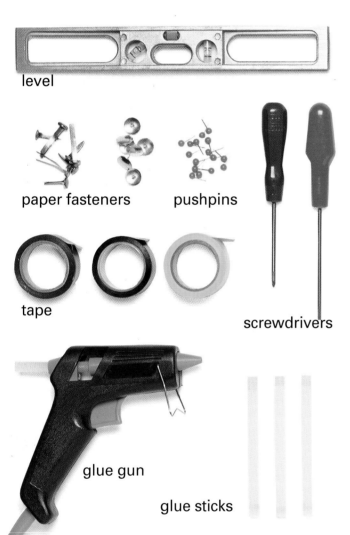

level

paper fasteners    pushpins

tape

screwdrivers

glue gun

glue sticks

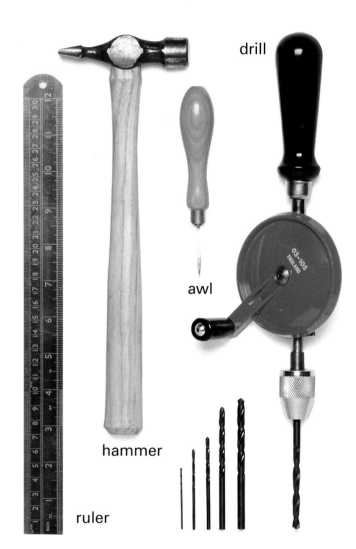

drill

awl

hammer

ruler

The scientists who build machines are called **engineers**. They do tests and experiments that help them to invent new machines and make old ones work better. Without engineers we wouldn't have tools or engines, trucks or trains, or even clocks or can openers.

## You will need

You can build most of your machines out of simple materials, such as cardboard and balsa wood, plastic bottles, and other odds and ends. However, you will need some tools to cut, shape, and join the different materials. All of the equipment shown above will come in very handy as part of an engineer's tool kit.

## Safety!

Sharp tools are dangerous! Always be careful when you use them, and ask an adult to help you. Make sure that anything you are cutting or drilling is held firmly so it cannot slip. A small table vise is ideal for holding pieces of wood.

## Planning and measuring

Always plan your machines carefully before starting to build. Measure the parts and mark them with a pencil before you cut. Mark the positions of holes before drilling them.

## Cutting

You will need saws for cutting wood and scissors for cutting cardboard and paper. A craft knife is useful too, but be careful with the sharp blade. After cutting, use sandpaper or a file to round off sharp edges.

## Drilling

To make some of the machines in this book, you will have to drill holes in pieces of wood. Use a pointed awl to start a hole and then finish it off neatly with a hand drill.

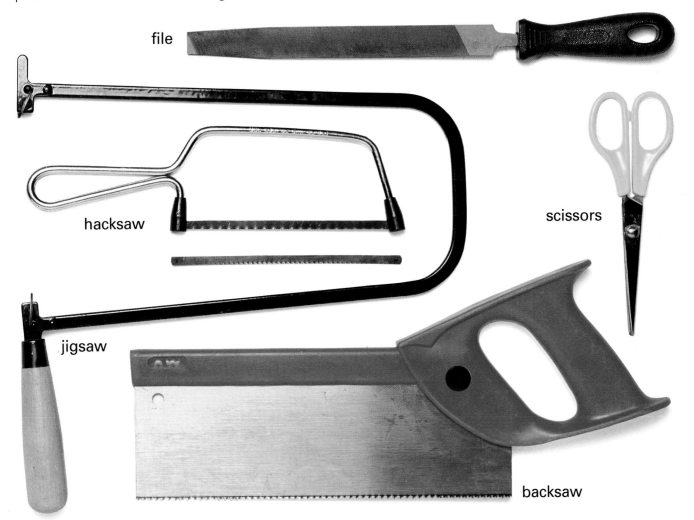

file

hacksaw

scissors

jigsaw

backsaw

## Joining

Strong glue is one of the simplest ways of joining pieces of wood, cardboard, or plastic. It's easiest to use glue sticks with a glue gun. Pushpins, paper fasteners, a hammer and nails, staples, and tape are all useful too. A level will come in handy if you want to make sure that parts are joined straight or level.

*Some machines are so simple that we don't always realize they are machines. But in fact, a machine is anything that applies a force to do a useful job. A pencil sharpener, for example, is a machine that uses a turning force to cut wood. Nutcrackers are machines that use a squeezing force to crack nuts.*

We often use machines to lift heavy weights or to help us move loads from one place to another. A wheelbarrow, for example, is a simple type of lifting machine. We use it to increase the **force** made by our muscles. If you had to move a pile of earth, you could carry a much heavier load in a wheelbarrow than you could lift in your own arms.

Perhaps the simplest machine of all for increasing force is the **lever**. A wheelbarrow is a kind of lever – and many other types of complicated machine are really just collections of levers that are put together to work in different ways.

effort

### To make a seesaw you will need

| | |
|---|---|
| a length of wood | glue |
| a small wooden dowel | a ruler |
| strips of colored paper | a pencil |
| weights (washers or coins) | a matchbox |

## MAKE it WORK!

A simple lever is a straight rod that rests on a **pivot** or **fulcrum**. When you push one end of the rod down with an **effort**, the other end goes up, lifting the **load**.

Try making this model seesaw and find out for yourself how levers work.

**1** Mark the length of wood with paper strips spaced about 1 inch apart.

**2** Glue the dowel to the matchbox to make a pivot.

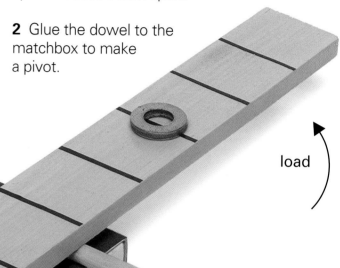

load

pivot or fulcrum

**3** Place the center of the length of wood on the pivot so that the two ends balance.

Now try some experiments with the weights. Put a weight (the load) three marks from the fulcrum. Where must you place another weight (the effort) to lift the load?

### More load for less effort!

If the load is close to the fulcrum, it's easier to lift and you don't need so much effort. You may have noticed this if you've ever played on a seesaw – you can lift someone heavier than yourself if they sit nearer to the middle than you do.

Try putting two weights (the load) two marks away from the fulcrum of your seesaw. Where must you put a single weight to lift the load?

## Scales

Weighing scales use a balancing lever to make delicate measurements. Try building these scales. They are sensitive enough to weigh even a feather!

### You will need

cardboard and tape
thread and nails
a strip of wood
modeling clay
a short dowel
two glasses
pins

**5** Rest the scale on the upturned glasses. If the two pans are not level, add small pieces of modeling clay to one of the pans until they balance exactly.

◀ Use your scales to weigh any light objects. How many pushpin weights do you need to balance a feather?

*A bottle opener is a lever. You can't open bottles with your bare hands! Can you see where the fulcrum, load, and effort are in this simple machine?*

**1** Ask an adult to help you cut a slot in the dowel and glue the wood strip into the slot.

**2** Hammer two nails through the dowel, one at each end as shown above.

**3** Make the scale pans with squares of cardboard, thread, and tape.

**4** Cut a notch at each end of the balance, and hang a pan from it.

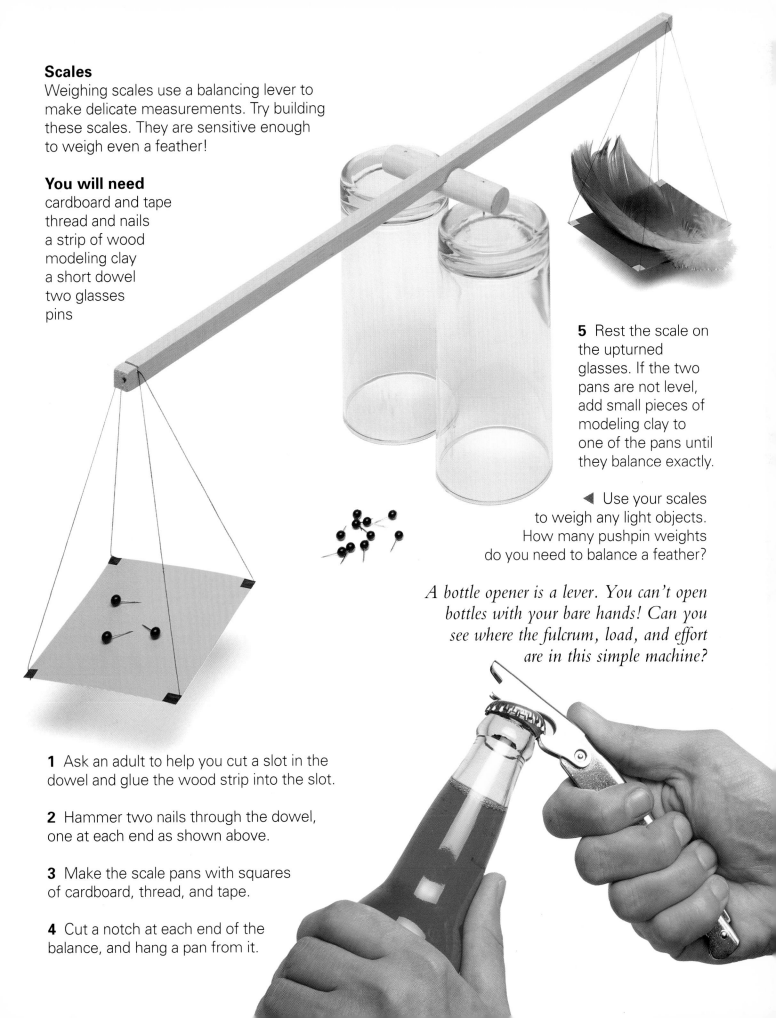

Have you ever flicked a pea from the end of a spoon? If you have, then you were using a lever. Your thumb was the pivot and your fingers applied the effort, making the bowl of the spoon move quickly and launching the pea up into the air.

A catapult works in just the same way. Before gunpowder was invented, ancient armies used catapults to fire rocks, burning rags, or other **projectiles** at their enemies.

**1** Ask an adult to help you cut the baseboard, the two side arms, and the main catapult arm from lengths of wood.

**2** Drill holes 1 inch apart along the main catapult arm and the side arms. The holes should be just big enough for the dowel to fit through. Before drilling, mark the position of each hole with an awl, as shown above.

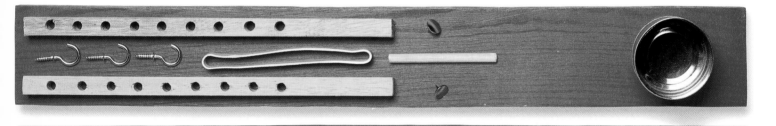

**MAKE it WORK!**
The catapult on this page is powered by a stretched rubber band.

**3** Cut the triangular side pieces out of corrugated cardboard. You will need to use a sharp knife, so be careful not to cut yourself.

**You will need**
a small tin can or plastic cup
thick corrugated cardboard    paint
a thick rubber band          an awl
strong wood glue             pushpins
pieces of sponge             screw hooks
a hand drill                 a wooden dowel
wood                         a sharp craft knife

**4** Glue the cardboard side pieces and the wooden side arms to the baseboard. Then glue the small can or plastic cup to the end of the main catapult arm.

**5** Screw three hooks into the baseboard. Use the awl to mark the positions of the screws before you twist them in.

*When you fire an object from the catapult, it travels in a curved path called its **trajectory**. The distance the object travels is called its **range**. The range of the object and how high it goes depend on its speed and the angle from which it is launched.*

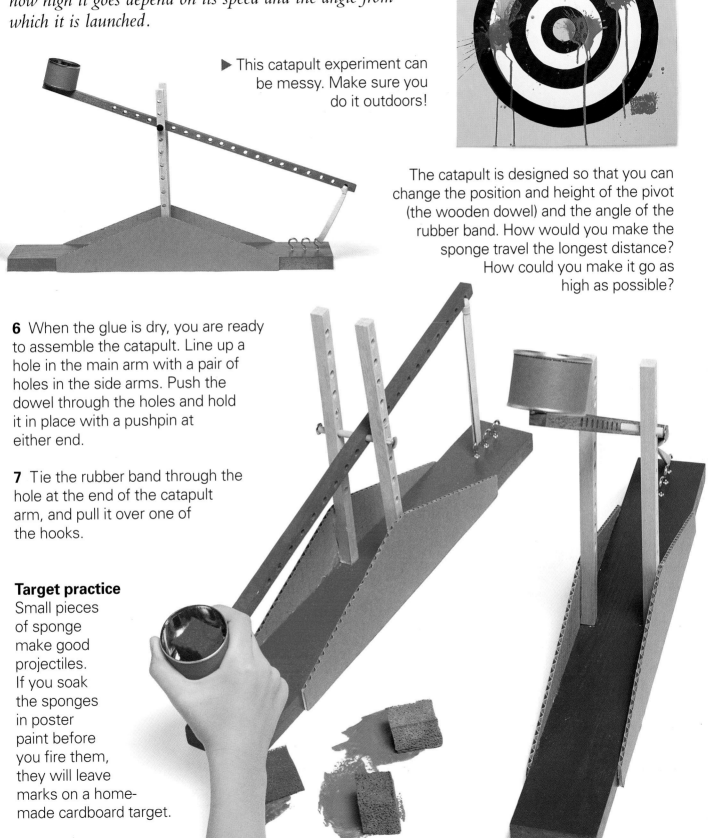

▶ This catapult experiment can be messy. Make sure you do it outdoors!

The catapult is designed so that you can change the position and height of the pivot (the wooden dowel) and the angle of the rubber band. How would you make the sponge travel the longest distance? How could you make it go as high as possible?

**6** When the glue is dry, you are ready to assemble the catapult. Line up a hole in the main arm with a pair of holes in the side arms. Push the dowel through the holes and hold it in place with a pushpin at either end.

**7** Tie the rubber band through the hole at the end of the catapult arm, and pull it over one of the hooks.

**Target practice**
Small pieces of sponge make good projectiles. If you soak the sponges in poster paint before you fire them, they will leave marks on a home-made cardboard target.

Lifting isn't the only job levers can do. We also use levers to change the direction of a movement.

The two ends of a simple lever always move in opposite directions. One end goes up when you push the other end down. By linking two levers with a flexible joint, we can make them move backward and forward as well as up and down. Bulldozers work in this way. The bones in our arms and legs are levers, connected at the knee and elbow joints.

**You will need**
glue
a cork
sandpaper
a hand drill
nuts and bolts
a pencil sharpener
lengths of balsa wood
a felt-tip pen and paper
a piece of wooden dowel
a drawing board and pushpins

## MAKE it WORK!
A pantograph is a drawing machine made from linked levers. Make one yourself and experiment to see how the linkages work.

**1** Cut two balsa wood lever arms 9 inches long and two more 5 inches long. Round the ends of the arms with sandpaper.

**2** Drill holes in the levers, just big enough for the bolts to fit through. Begin by making holes at the ends of all four levers.

**3** Now drill an extra hole in the middle of each of the two longer levers. If the pantograph is to work well, all the holes must be equally spaced – so be sure to measure carefully and mark the holes with a pencil before drilling.

**4** Join the longer levers at one end using a nut and bolt. Then attach a short lever to the middle of each long arm. Don't make the bolts too tight, since all the levers need to move freely.

**5** Ask an adult to help you drill a hole in the cork, just big enough for the pen to fit through.

**6** Glue the cork to the free end of one short lever. Push the pen through it and the free end of the other short arm as shown on the right.

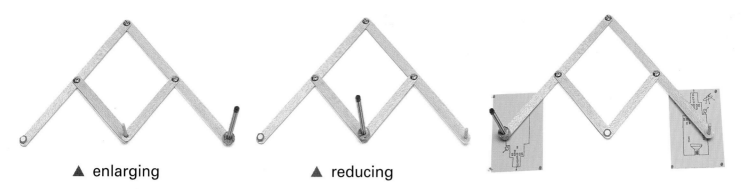

▲ enlarging      ▲ reducing

▲ drawing upside down

**7** Sharpen the piece of dowel to a point with a pencil sharpener and put it through the hole at the end of one of the long lever arms.

**8** Place the pantograph on a drawing board and push a pin through the last free hole.

**9** Pin the drawing you want to copy under the dowel pointer and put a blank piece of paper under the felt-tip pen.

**10** Trace around the drawing with the pointer and watch how the pantograph's lever arms carry the movement to the pen.

▼ With the pantograph set up like this, the copy is smaller than the original. The short arms are half the length of the long ones, so the copy is half the size.

### Different drawings

If you swap around the positions of the pin, wooden pointer, and felt-tip pen, you can also make the pantograph draw larger, or the same size but upside down. The photographs above show how you should arrange the parts to produce some of these different results with your pantograph.

### Pantograph experiments

What do you think would happen if you changed the length of the lever arms? You could experiment by drilling more holes along the arms and then bolting them together in different ways. You may end up with drawings that look stretched, squashed, or tilted!

*The movements made by linked levers depend on two things: the length of the levers and the positions of the joints. A movement can be made bigger or smaller simply by changing the way the lever rods are linked to one another.*

Imagine that you wanted to hang a flag from the top of a tall pole without moving your feet from the ground. How could you do it?

The easiest answer would be to use a **pulley**, attached to the top of the pole, with a rope looped over it.

A pulley changes a downward pull on one end of a rope into an upward pull at the other end. With simple pulleys we can lift all kinds of loads up poles or tall buildings – and if you have a window blind at home, you'll be using pulleys yourself every time you pull it up or down.

**MAKE it WORK!**
Thread spools make first-class pulley wheels. With a few spools you can make a whole set of pulleys to experiment with.

**You will need**
empty thread spools
string or cord
yogurt cups
thick wire
eyebolts
pliers
sand

▲ **Single pulley**
**1** Push a piece of wire through the hole in a thread spool. Use the pliers to cut, bend, and twist the wire to make a pulley as shown.

**2** Make sure the thread spool spins freely on the wire and then hang the pulley from an eyebolt.

**3** Loop the string over the pulley and tie a load to one end. A yogurt cup filled with sand is a good load. Push a wire through the sides of the cup to make the handle.

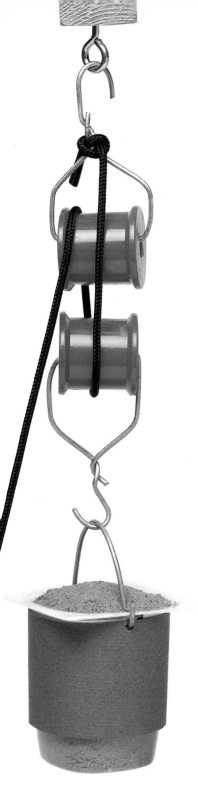

### Easing the load

Experiment to see how easily you can lift the cup full of sand with your simple pulley. One single pulley won't make it any easier to lift the load, it just changes the direction in which you apply the force. You pull down on the rope to make the load go up. With a single pulley you cannot lift anything heavier than you could using just the strength of your arms. However, see what happens if you use two or more pulley wheels together.

### ◀ Double pulley

**1** Make a second simple pulley just like the first, and hook it to the cup handle.

**2** Tie one end of the string to the top of the wire hanger on the first pulley as shown.

**3** Loop the string under the lower pulley and then back up over the top of the upper pulley.

Now test the double pulley system to feel how difficult it is to lift a load. Do you need to use more force than with a single pulley, or less?

### ▶ Quadruple pulley

To make a pulley system with four wheels you will need to make two twin **pulley blocks**.

**1** Using a longer piece of wire, make two new hangers, each wide enough to hold two thread spools, positioned side by side.

**2** Tie the string to the top hanger. Loop it down under one of the lower pulleys and then around each of the other pulleys as shown.

How does this system of four pulley reels compare to the simpler ones?

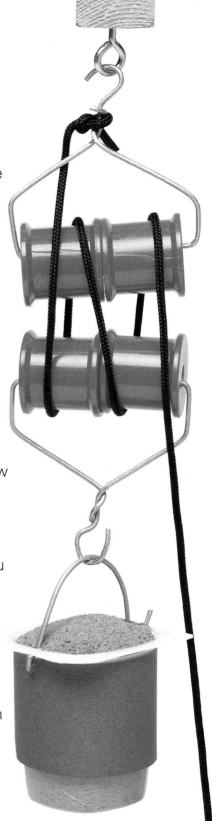

### Heavier weights, shorter distances

With two pulleys you can lift almost twice as much as with a single pulley, without using any extra force. But you don't get anything for nothing – the load only travels up half as far as the distance you pull on the string! Four pulleys lift almost four times as much weight.

*Pulley systems work in about the same way as levers. They help us to lift big loads with just a small effort. With a pulley block, a car mechanic can lift the engine out of a car in order to repair or replace it.*

Have you ever been ice-skating? Skates glide smoothly across the ice and you move with hardly any effort. Rubber boots, on the other hand, are not slippery at all. They keep a firm grip on the ground, and keep you from sliding even if you're walking in slippery mud.

▲ Put some marbles under a pan lid on a smooth surface. The marbles cut down the friction, and the lid rolls around smoothly. Balls that reduce friction in this way are called **ball bearings**.

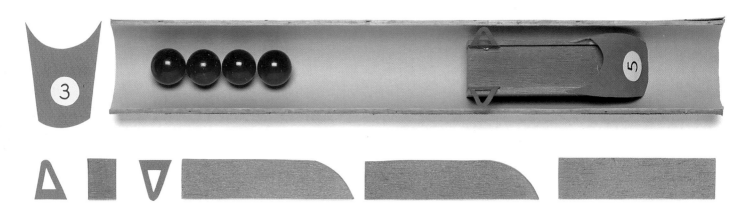

## Friction
Rubber boots grip the ground firmly because of **friction**. This is an invisible force, caused when two objects rub against one another. Friction keeps things from sliding. When rubber rubs against anything, it causes lots of friction. But thin strips of metal on ice make hardly any friction at all.

## Bearings
Friction can be a nuisance in machines, and it may keep the parts from moving smoothly. Many machines contain ball bearings to cut down on friction. There are ball bearings inside the **hub** of a bicycle wheel. As the wheel rotates, the steel balls turn around inside the hub.

## MAKE it WORK!

At the Winter Olympics, bobsleds hurtle down the icy bobsled run at thrilling speeds. These model bobsleds don't run on ice – but they can still pick up plenty of speed as they race down their tracks of cardboard.

### You will need

strong wood glue
cardboard tubes
wooden dowels
thin cardboard
some marbles
modeling clay
balsa wood

**4** Build a track from sections of tube that are connected with curves of fairly thin cardboard. Hold the track up on pieces of wooden dowel connected with lumps of modeling clay.

**5** Decorate your track with cardboard flags and colored markers.

**6** Place the bobsled on the marbles and set it off down the run. The marbles don't make much friction, so the sled picks up speed and will be going fast once it reaches the bottom!

**1** Cut out the balsa wood pieces to make the sides, top, and back of the bobsled. The bobsled should be slightly wider than the marbles, but not quite as deep.

**2** Glue the balsa wood parts together. Cut the nose and the tail fins from thin cardboard and glue them in place.

**3** Ask an adult to help you cut some cardboard tubes in half lengthwise. (The insides of old aluminum foil rolls come in handy here, or, if you have some old plastic gutters, you could even use them to make the bobsled track.)

### Bobsled races

Build a double run, make two bobsleds, and you can hold competitions. Try adding weights to the sleds (use lumps of clay) – do the weights make the sleds go faster?

*Ball bearings aren't the only way of cutting down friction. Oil is a good solution, too. The slippery liquid spreads out in a very thin layer between the moving parts of a machine. Oil is a vital part of most **engines**.*

Merry-go-rounds, sewing machines, record players, fishing reels, washing machines, and bicycles: these are just a few of the many machines that turn, or **rotate,** as they work.

All the different rotating parts inside a machine can be connected with a **drive belt.** As one part turns, it drags the belt around with it, carrying its turning motion to all the other parts of the machine.

**1** Cut the sandpaper into strips, and glue a strip around each of the thread spools. The rough surface of the sandpaper is needed to make some friction between the reels and the belt. This way, the belt will not slip.

**2** Draw both the front and the back of each acrobat on a piece of cardboard as shown, leaving a space between front and back to make a base. Cut out the figures. Then fold and glue them so that they stand up.

**3** Glue an acrobat onto each spool.

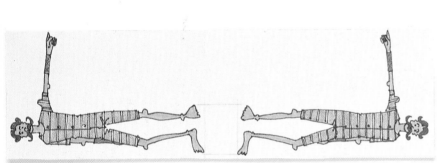
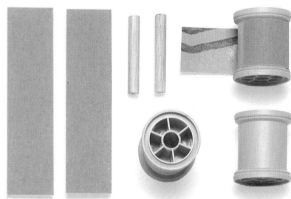

## MAKE it WORK!

A drive belt runs around a series of pulleys to carry the turning force from one place to another. If the belt is going to work properly, there must be **friction** between it and the pulleys, so that the belt does not slip. If the belt is too slack, it will not grip. If it is too tight, it might break or twist the pulleys out of line. These whirling acrobats stand on thread spools connected by a belt made of ribbon.

### You will need
sandpaper
a wooden board                    empty thread spools
glue and cardboard                    a wooden dowel
a piece of hook-and-loop fasteners          a ribbon

**4** Ask an adult to help you cut the wooden dowel into a number of shorter dowel pegs. Smooth the ends of the pegs with sandpaper.

**5** Drill holes into the baseboard. They should be just big enough for the dowel pegs to fit snugly into them.

**6** Put the pegs into the holes, and then put a thread spool onto each peg. Make sure that every reel can turn freely on its peg.

**7** Push a short piece of dowel into the gap between the center hole and the rim of one thread spool. This is the drive belt handle. You will use it to turn the drive belt.

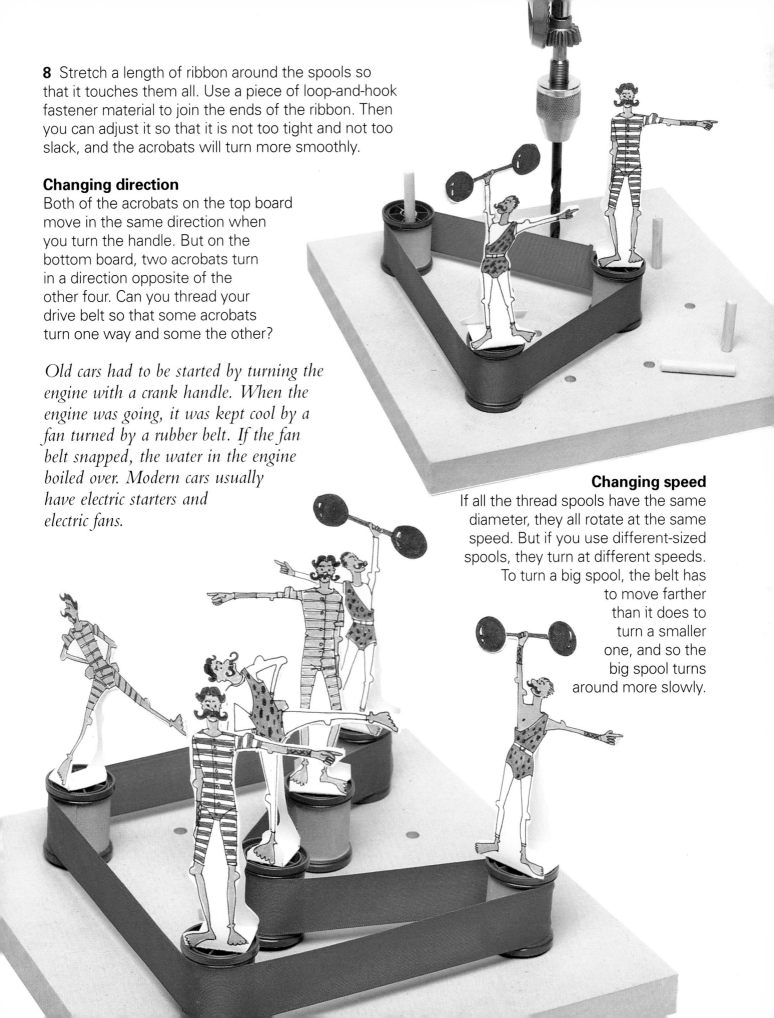

**8** Stretch a length of ribbon around the spools so that it touches them all. Use a piece of loop-and-hook fastener material to join the ends of the ribbon. Then you can adjust it so that it is not too tight and not too slack, and the acrobats will turn more smoothly.

## Changing direction

Both of the acrobats on the top board move in the same direction when you turn the handle. But on the bottom board, two acrobats turn in a direction opposite of the other four. Can you thread your drive belt so that some acrobats turn one way and some the other?

*Old cars had to be started by turning the engine with a crank handle. When the engine was going, it was kept cool by a fan turned by a rubber belt. If the fan belt snapped, the water in the engine boiled over. Modern cars usually have electric starters and electric fans.*

## Changing speed

If all the thread spools have the same diameter, they all rotate at the same speed. But if you use different-sized spools, they turn at different speeds. To turn a big spool, the belt has to move farther than it does to turn a smaller one, and so the big spool turns around more slowly.

You'll find **gears** inside nearly every machine that turns. Clocks, watches, and bicycles all use them. Just like a belt drive, the gears connect all of the rotating parts, but gears last longer than belts and are more precise. If you've ever ridden a mountain bike, you'll know that gears are a good way of changing speed too.

## MAKE it WORK!

The best way to find out how gears work is to make some of your own to experiment with. Each of these homemade gears is made from a jar lid with a strip of corrugated cardboard stuck around the rim. The corrugations face out to make the gear teeth.

**1** Bend a strip of cardboard around the rim of a jar lid. Try to stretch it into place so that there is a whole number of teeth evenly spaced around the lid. Cut the strip carefully to length and then glue it in place.

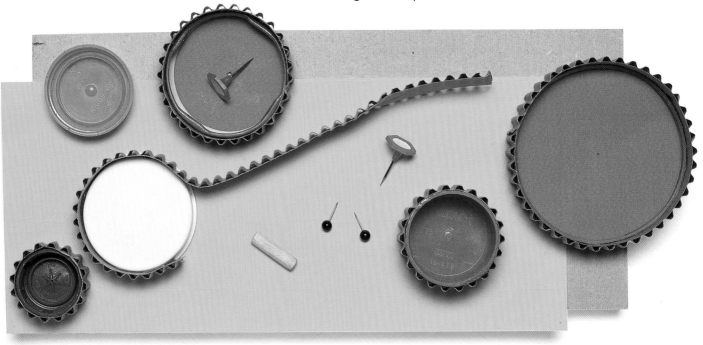

### You will need
strips of corrugated cardboard about ½ inch
  wide (You can make these by peeling apart
  the thick cardboard sides of a cardboard box.)
jar lids and bottle tops of different sizes
a pin board and pushpins
a short dowel peg
glue and paper

**2** Make a small hole in the middle of the gear and pin it to the board so that it spins freely.

**3** Make a selection of different-sized gears to add to the board. Glue a dowel peg to one of the gears to make a crank handle.

**4** To make the gears work you must place them so the teeth **mesh**. When you turn one gear its teeth will push on its neighbor's teeth and make them turn in the opposite direction.

## Gear experiments

Connect a series of gears like the one shown above. If you turn the big gear, what happens to the two smaller ones? Which way do they go around? Which does a complete turn first?

Now try turning the small gear – do the bigger gears turn more quickly or more slowly?

Count the number of teeth on each gear. If you turned a gear with 20 teeth around once, how many times would it turn a gear with 10 teeth?

## Drive chains

In some machines, gears called **sprockets** are connected by a **drive chain**. A bicycle chain connects a sprocket on the pedals to another one on the back wheel. The chain transfers the movement from the pedals to the wheels.

▼ Make a model drive chain from a long strip of corrugated cardboard with the ends taped together. Loop it around two different-sized gears and work out how far the small gear moves when you turn the larger one.

Turning gears make beautiful patterns. As a gear goes around, each point on the wheel's surface follows a different path. By tracing these paths, we can draw patterns of loops and curves that repeat and shift as the gear rotates.

**1** Use a craft knife to cut a large, circular hole in a square of stiff cardboard.

**2** Glue a narrow strip of corrugated cardboard around the inside of the hole. Position the strip so that the corrugations face into the hole to make gear teeth. Make sure that one edge of the strip is level with the edge of the hole, so that the cardboard will lie flat on top of the pin board.

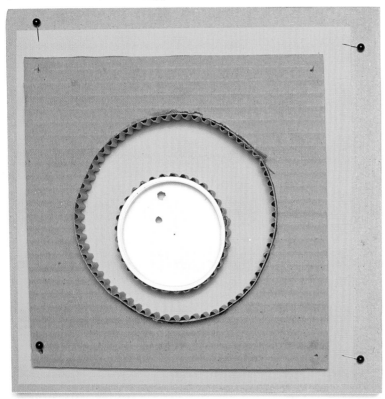

### MAKE it WORK!
This gear drawing machine uses the homemade lid and corrugated cardboard gears from the page before. Experiment with different-sized gears to discover all kinds of patterns.

### You will need
pushpins
a pin board
corrugated cardboard
gears made from lids and cardboard (Plastic lids are easiest to make holes in.)
drawing paper
a pen or pencil

**3** Put a sheet of paper on the pin board and then pin the square with the hole in it on top.

**4** Make small holes in your gear wheels at different distances from the center. The holes must be big enough for the point of your pen to fit through.

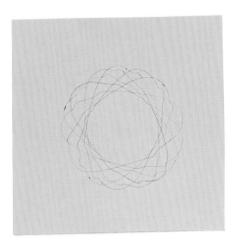
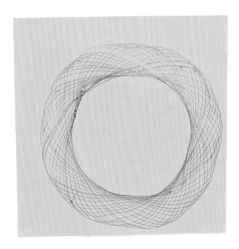

**5** Place a gear wheel in the large cardboard hole and put the point of a pen through one of the small holes so it touches the paper.

**6** Hold the board firmly with one hand and use the pen to push the gear carefully around the inside of the large circle. As the gear rotates, the pen draws a line on the paper.

**7** Keep pushing the pen and the gear around to build up a beautiful curved pattern.

▲ Try to make some drawings using different-sized gears and with holes that are at different distances from the center of the gear.

Some patterns will repeat after just a few turns, others may take many turns before they start again. Think about how the number of teeth on the gears and the position of the pen hole affect the pattern. You could also make up a second gear board with a different-sized hole to investigate even more patterns.

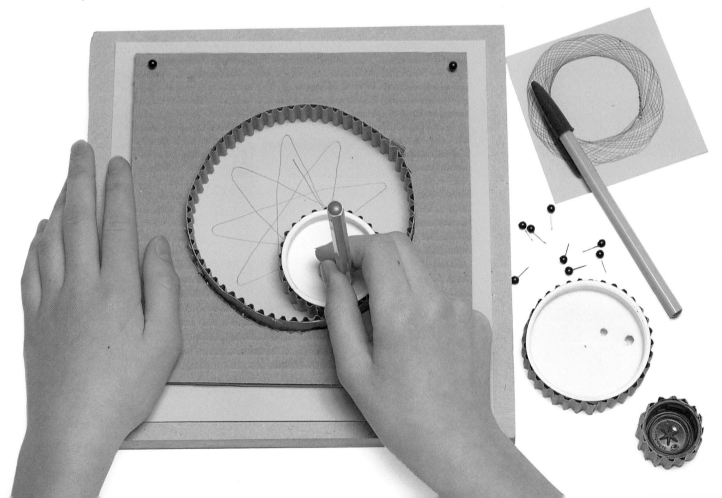

Gears let us transfer movement from one wheel to another, but how do you change a turning movement into an up and down one? The answer is a **cam**.

A cam is like a wheel, but with the **axle** (the shaft that goes through the middle) off center. If you watch a point on the edge of the cam, it seems to move up and down as the axle of the cam goes around and around.

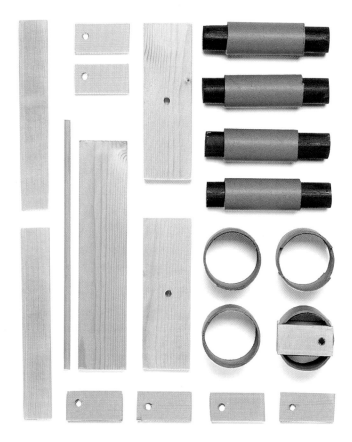

## MAKE it WORK!
This model camshaft shows exactly how rotating cams can move things up and down – and in the order you choose.

### You will need
| | |
|---|---|
| wood | a small tack |
| strong wood glue | thick and thin dowels |
| two thick cardboard tubes of different widths | |

**1** Ask an adult to help you cut the pieces of wood needed for the frame which will hold the camshaft and the four plungers. The height of the frame must be at least twice the diameter of the cams. The plunger tubes must fit tightly into the space across the top of the frame.

**2** Cut the wide cardboard tube into four rings. These will be your cams.

**3** Cut eight short strips of wood that just fit across the cardboard cams. At the end of each strip, drill a hole with a diameter a little larger than that of the thin dowel rod.

**4** Cut slots in the rims of the cams and glue the wooden strips in place as shown. Make sure the holes face each other on opposite sides of each cam.

**5** When the glue is dry, push the cams onto the dowel rod to complete the camshaft.

**6** Cut four pieces of the narrow cardboard tube and four longer pieces of the fatter dowel to fit inside. These will be the plungers.

**7** Drill two holes, facing one another, halfway down each of the frame's side pieces.

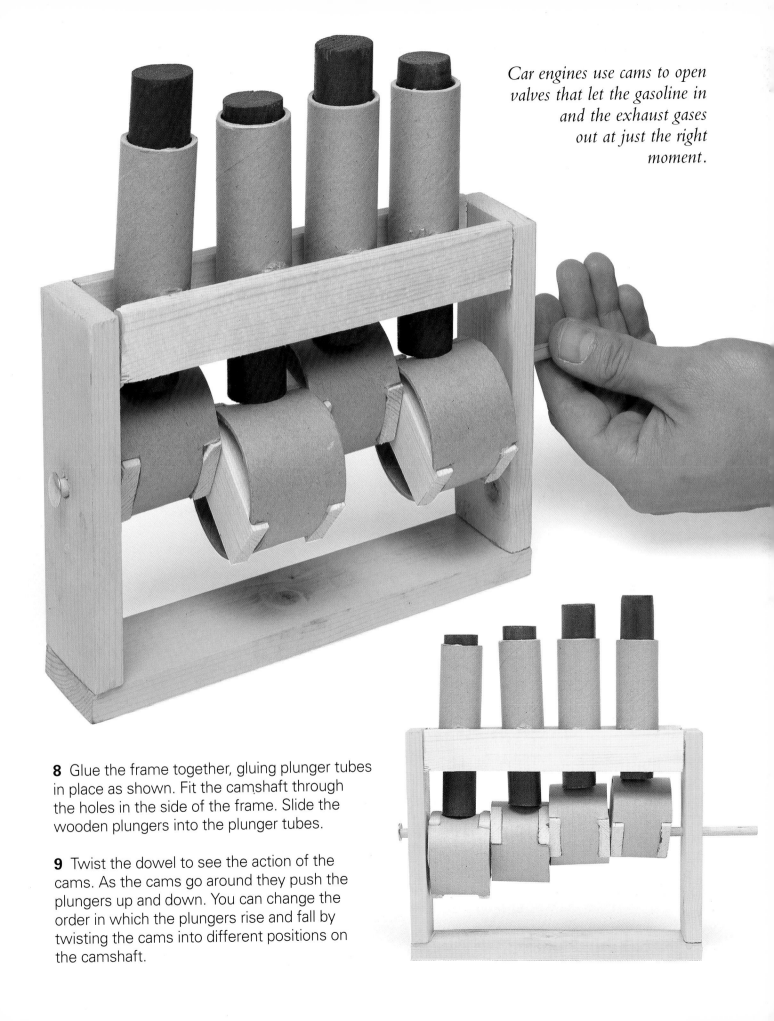

*Car engines use cams to open valves that let the gasoline in and the exhaust gases out at just the right moment.*

**8** Glue the frame together, gluing plunger tubes in place as shown. Fit the camshaft through the holes in the side of the frame. Slide the wooden plungers into the plunger tubes.

**9** Twist the dowel to see the action of the cams. As the cams go around they push the plungers up and down. You can change the order in which the plungers rise and fall by twisting the cams into different positions on the camshaft.

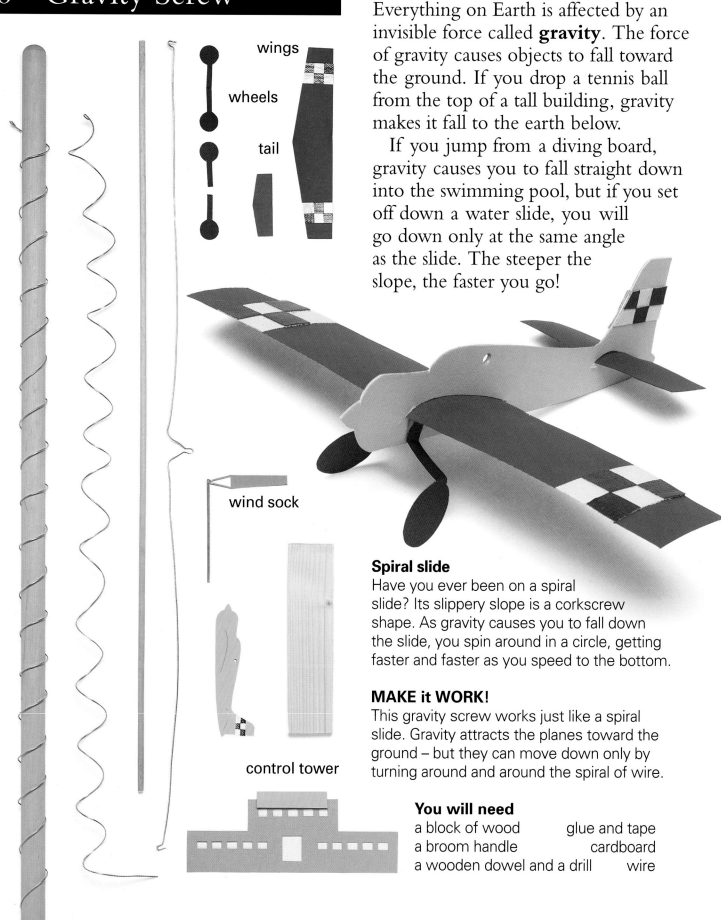

wings

wheels

tail

Everything on Earth is affected by an invisible force called **gravity**. The force of gravity causes objects to fall toward the ground. If you drop a tennis ball from the top of a tall building, gravity makes it fall to the earth below.

If you jump from a diving board, gravity causes you to fall straight down into the swimming pool, but if you set off down a water slide, you will go down only at the same angle as the slide. The steeper the slope, the faster you go!

wind sock

control tower

## Spiral slide
Have you ever been on a spiral slide? Its slippery slope is a corkscrew shape. As gravity causes you to fall down the slide, you spin around in a circle, getting faster and faster as you speed to the bottom.

## MAKE it WORK!
This gravity screw works just like a spiral slide. Gravity attracts the planes toward the ground – but they can move down only by turning around and around the spiral of wire.

### You will need
| | |
|---|---|
| a block of wood | glue and tape |
| a broom handle | cardboard |
| a wooden dowel and a drill | wire |

**1** Wind a length of wire around the broom handle to make the spiral. Take care to make the loops of the spiral evenly spaced. Slide the finished spiral off the handle.

**2** Ask an adult to help you drill a hole in the block of wood. Glue the dowel in the hole.

**3** Slip the wire spiral over the dowel. Use a piece of tape to hold it in place on the block.

**4** Make a cardboard wind sock and control tower, and then glue them to the block.

**5** Cut out the parts for the two cardboard planes. Make two slits in the body and slide the wings and tail through each. Glue the wheels under the wings.

**6** Gently hold the body of one plane between your thumb and finger to find the place where it balances. Make a small hole in the body at this point.

**7** Bend a second length of wire into a hanger shape. Make a loop in the middle to fit over the wire spiral and bend small hooks at each end.

**8** Hang the planes on the hooks and put the hanger on the top of the spiral. Let it go, and see if it runs smoothly down the spiral. You may need to adjust the shape of the hanger loop and some of the twists in the spiral to get the planes to fly really well.

*The seeds of the sycamore tree grow in pairs. Each seed has a wing attached, which makes every pair spin around as it falls out of the tree. The spinning movement slows down the fall of the seeds, so that they catch the wind and travel farther away from the tree before finally settling on the ground.*

Spirals and screws come in handy for moving things up as well as down. One of the first people to use a screw as a lifting machine was the ancient Greek scientist Archimedes. He invented a screw pump that could raise water from a lower level up to a higher one, making it flow against the force of gravity.

## MAKE it WORK!

This model Archimedean screw is not really strong enough, or made of the right materials, to lift water, but it is an ideal dispenser for popcorn or breakfast cereal.

### You will need

a wooden dowel
a sharp craft knife
a plastic soft drink bottle

glue
a small tack
stiff cardboard

**1** Ask an adult to help you cut the bottom off the bottle and to cut a triangular hole in the neck as shown.

**2** Cut out six cardboard disks, just big enough to fit inside the plastic bottle.

**3** Cut a small hole in the center of each disk, the same diameter as the wooden dowel.

**4** Make a slit in each cardboard disk, from the center hole to the edge.

**5** Now join the cardboard disks to make the screw shape. Take two disks. Glue the edge of the slit in one disk onto the opposite edge of the slit in the second disk.

**6** Next, glue the free edge of the slit in the second disk to the opposite edge of the slit in a third disk.

**7** Continue to glue the slit edges in this way until all six disks have been stuck together to make a screw.

**8** Push the dowel through the holes in the centers of the disks, and stretch out the screw along the length of the dowel as shown below. Glue the two free ends of the cardboard screw firmly to the dowel.

**9** Slide the completed screw into the bottle. Hold it in place with a small tack pushed through the bottle cap and into the end of the wooden dowel.

**10** Now test your Archimedean screw. Dip the bottle into a bowl of popcorn and twist the dowel gently with your fingers to draw some popcorn up out of the bowl.

*Archimedean screws are used in combine harvesters to lift grain into storage containers.*

▲ Just like cams, screws are a way of changing one kind of movement into another. Our popcorn dispenser changes rotation (twisting the dowel) into upward movement.

*Although Archimedean screws were first built more than two thousand years ago, they are still used today. In some parts of Africa, farmers use them for irrigating their crops. The screws lift water out of rivers into raised irrigation canals. These ancient water pumps are powered either by animals or by hand.*

Because gravity attracts things toward the ground, it is much simpler to stay on a trapeze than it is to balance on a high wire. A trapeze artist's weight hangs below her hands, so as long as she has strong arms and holds on tight, she won't fall off. But a tightrope walker's weight is all above her feet – she only has to lean over a little and she topples from the wire.

▲ A **pendulum** bob hangs
with its weight as low as possible. If you push it aside, the force of gravity brings it back again.

## MAKE it WORK!
Try making these simple balancing toys. They seem to stand above the wire, but they work because really most of their weight is hanging below it.

### To make balancing acrobats you will need
| | |
|---|---|
| stiff cardboard | colored pens |
| small metal washers | glue and scissors |

**1** Draw an acrobat on a piece of cardboard. The left-hand side should be a mirror image of the right.

**2** Cut out the acrobat. Cut a small notch in his hat where he will balance on the wire.

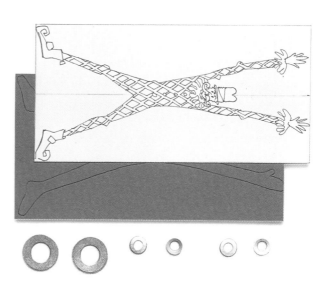

**3** Glue a washer to each of the acrobat's hands.

The weight of the washers below the wire helps the acrobats to balance above it.

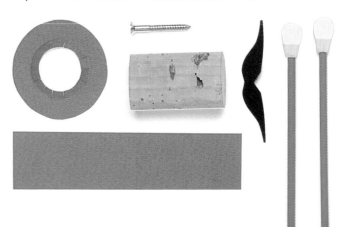

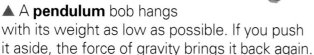

*Some tightrope walkers carry a long, flexible pole. It helps to keep their weight low, just like the mustache men's knitting needles.*

## Gyroscopes

A gyroscope is a machine that seems to defy the force of gravity. It has a heavy metal disk, which spins around on an axle inside a frame. Although gravity still attracts the machine down, the spinning movement of the disk stops it from toppling over, and so the gyroscope balances on the wire.

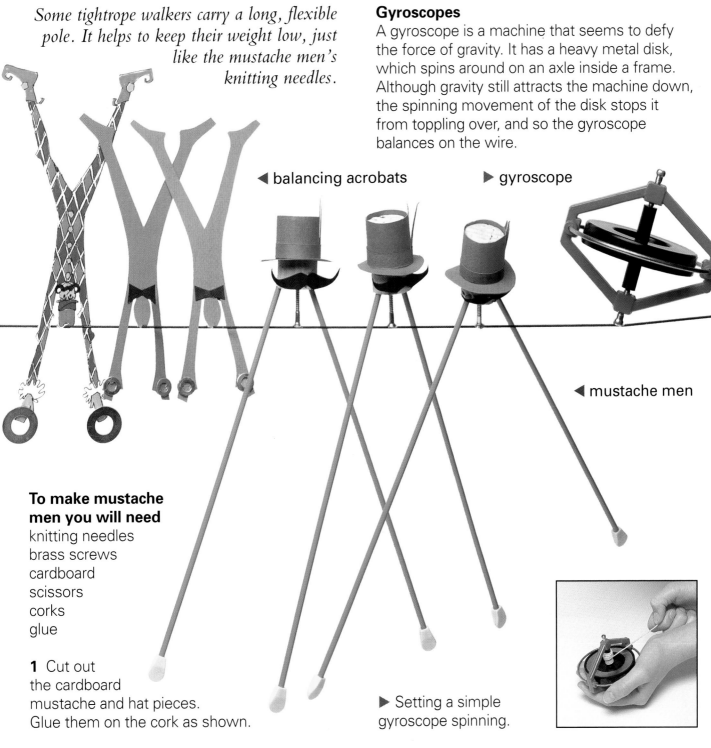

◄ balancing acrobats　　▶ gyroscope

◄ mustache men

**To make mustache men you will need**
knitting needles
brass screws
cardboard
scissors
corks
glue

**1** Cut out the cardboard mustache and hat pieces. Glue them on the cork as shown.

**2** Twist a screw into the bottom of the cork.

**3** Ask an adult to help you push two knitting needles into the cork at an angle.

Just like the acrobats, the mustache men balance because most of their weight is in the knitting needles, below the wire.

▶ Setting a simple gyroscope spinning.

*A gyroscope has a very useful feature – once it is spinning, the axle will keep on pointing in the same direction as long as it is allowed to move freely. In the early twentieth century, scientists used this feature to develop a new kind of compass – the* **gyrocompass***, which is used in most ships and aircraft today.*

**Pneumatic** machines use air to transfer force from one place to another. We tend to think that air is weak and thin, but if it is squashed together, or **compressed**, it can push with tremendous strength. A hurricane, for instance, can blow down trees and buildings. The air inside an air mattress will hold up the weight of a person. And a tire filled with air can carry the weight of a huge truck or a jumbo jet.

## MAKE it WORK!

This pneumatic man is fired by squeezing the plastic bottle to compress the air inside. The air is pushed out along the straw and launches the flyer like a human cannonball.

### You will need

a liquid detergent bottle
cardboard and thread
a plastic bag
a thin straw
a fat straw
tape

**1** Seal one end of the fat straw with a piece of tape.

**2** Cut out the shape of the man in thin cardboard and stick him to the sealed end of the straw.

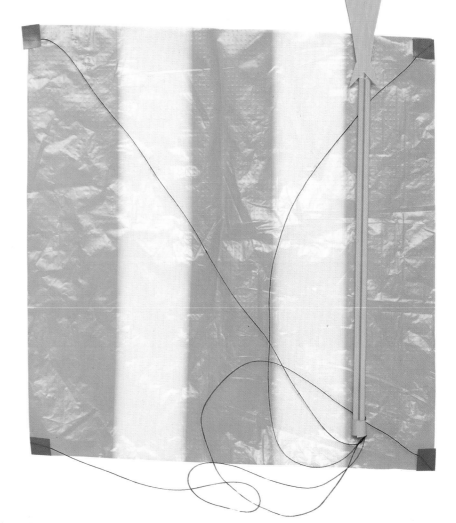

**3** Push the thin straw onto the nozzle of the dishwashing liquid bottle. If it does not fit very well, seal the join with modeling clay or glue.

**4** Slide the fat straw over the thin straw. If the fat straw doesn't fit neatly, cut a slit up its side and pull it a little tighter around the thinner straw. Then seal it up again with tape.

**5** To test the pneumatic man, squeeze the bottle sharply. The compressed air inside the bottle pushes against the sealed end of the thick straw as it tries to get out. The flying man is launched along a curved **trajectory**, like the sponges launched from the catapult on page 11.

### Parachute

If your man is a high-flyer, you could equip him with a parachute so that he has a soft landing.

### Pneumatic tires

Pneumatic tires are tires filled with compressed air. Before these tires were invented, carts and bicycles had simple tires made from solid rubber strips. Pneumatic tires are a great improvement because they are springier, so they give a much more comfortable ride than solid rubber.

*Pneumatic tires were invented by John Dunlop in 1888. He had the idea for them when he saw his son riding a tricycle over a piece of rough ground. Dunlop made his first air-filled tire from a length of rubber garden hose. The company he founded still makes tires today.*

**1** Cut a 7 inch square sheet from a plastic bag.

**2** Tape an equal length of thread to each corner of the plastic square. Then tape all the free ends of thread to the base of the fat straw.

**3** Fold the parachute into a strip and lay it alongside the straw.

**4** Launch the man in the usual way. The parachute will unfold and bring him gently back down to the ground.

▶ As it comes down, the open parachute fills with air. Air pushing upward underneath the plastic slows down the man's fall, just as it would slow the fall of a tissue or feather.

All machines need **energy** to make them go. Our pulleys were turned by human muscle energy. The gravity screw worked by the downward force of gravity on the plane. But most big machines today are driven by **engines**.

An engine makes power by burning a fuel such as gasoline or coal. Burning the fuel releases the energy it contains. A rocket engine works by burning the rocket fuel so that it squirts hot gases backward at great speed. As the gases push back, the rocket is thrust forward and shoots up into the sky.

### MAKE it WORK!

This water rocket isn't powered by rocket fuel, but it does work in a way similar to a real rocket by using just air and water. The space above the water is pumped full of compressed air with a bicycle pump. Eventually, the energy stored in the squashed air pushes the water out of the base, and the rocket is thrust up off the ground.

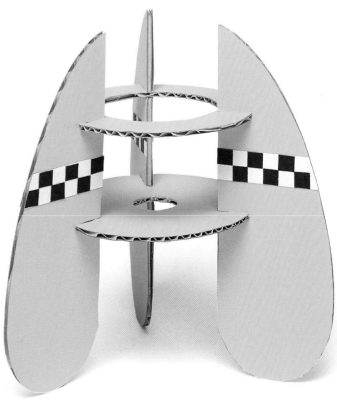

**To make a water rocket you will need**

| | |
|---|---|
| strong glue | tape |
| a bicycle pump | a rubber stopper or cork |
| a plastic bottle | thick, corrugated cardboard |

an air valve (The kind that is used for blowing up footballs is best – you can buy one at a sporting goods store.)

## Be very careful!

This rocket is very powerful and could hurt people seriously if it hit them. **Never** launch it without an adult to help you.

- **Always** fly the rocket out of doors in a wide empty space, well away from roads.
- **Never** fly the rocket near other people.
- **Don't** stand over the rocket as you pump it up. Keep off to the side.

**1** Cut the three base fins, two base rings, and three nose cone parts from corrugated cardboard.

**2** Make the rocket base from the fins and the two rings as shown. Stick the parts together with tape or strong glue. Then glue the base onto the plastic bottle.

**3** Make the nose cone and attach it to the top of the rocket.

**4** Ask an adult to help you make a small hole through the rubber stopper with a pin or a skewer. Then push the air valve through the stopper.

**5** Choose your launch site carefully. (See the safety note above.)

**6** Pour water into the bottle until it is about one-third full. Push the stopper tightly into the neck of the bottle and stand the rocket on its base. Attach the bicycle pump to the air valve, stand off to the side, and start pumping.

◀ As you pump, you will see the bubbles of air rising through the water. The pressure builds up inside the bottle until the stopper can no longer hold in place. Suddenly, the rocket blasts off, squirting out water as it lifts into the sky.

A windmill uses the force of the wind to do useful work. Waterwheels turn the energy of running water into useful power. Before the first steam engines were invented, windmills and water-wheels were almost the only machines that were not powered by human or animal muscles. Farmers often used them to grind corn and pump water.

## MAKE it WORK!

Try making this simple windmill. The wind turns a crank, which makes a rod go up and down.

### You will need

| | |
|---|---|
| a wooden dowel | wood |
| strong wood glue | a drill |
| a sharp craft knife | a cork |
| strips of thin plastic | cardboard |
| a tube of thick cardboard | wire and beads |

**1** Cut four strips of wood to length to make the frame. Bend the wire crank to shape.

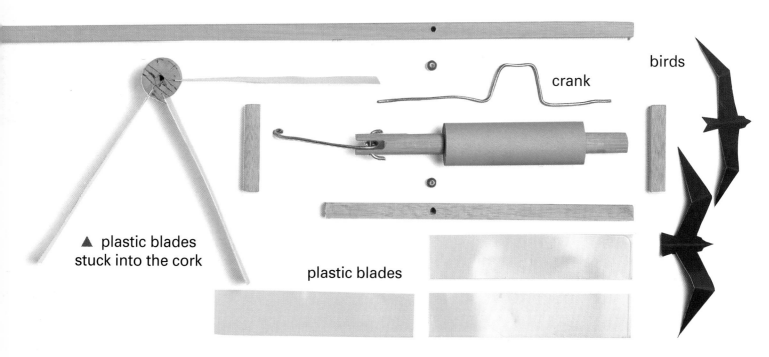

crank

birds

▲ plastic blades stuck into the cork

plastic blades

When engines fueled by coal and oil came along, windmills and water-wheels began to disappear. However, they are now becoming popular again. Today, we are more aware of the **pollution** caused by burning **fossil fuels** such as coal, gas, and oil. In comparison, wind and water power are clean and quiet sources of energy. They have another advantage, too — unlike coal, gas, and oil, our supplies of wind and water will never run out!

**2** Drill holes facing each other in the longer frame side pieces to take the crank. Glue the frame together with the crank in place.

**3** Ask an adult to help you cut slits in the cork. Slip the blades in place and secure with glue.

**4** Slip a bead over each end of the crank shaft. Then push the cork onto one end of the shaft. Bend the other end to keep the shaft in place.

**5** Cut a slot in one end of the dowel rod. Drill a hole at right angles to the slot and pass a small horseshoe-shaped wire through the hole.

**6** Glue the cardboard tube to the top of the frame and push the dowel through it. Connect the wire horseshoe to the crank with a third piece of wire as shown. Make sure the dowel moves up and down easily as the crank turns.

**7** Glue cardboard birds to the top of the dowel.

▶ Turn the mill by blowing a hair dryer at the blades. Experiment with the windmill out of doors too. Does it catch the wind better if you fit the blades into the cork at a different angle?

*Modern windmills don't just grind corn or pump water. Nowadays, engineers can also build windmills to generate electricity.*

## Water power

Waterwheels can be built wherever there is fast-flowing water that will turn the blades of the wheel. Most modern waterwheels are complicated machines that are used to make electricity. They are called **hydroelectric turbines** and the electricity they produce is **hydroelectricity**. Hydroelectric turbines are usually built along big rivers or in dams, where water is made to pass through a turbine in order to get out of a reservoir. Electricity can even be generated in coastal areas by the movement of the tides through a turbine.

▶ **Waterwheel**
Try designing your own simple waterwheel. This model has plastic blades fixed onto a cork, with a wooden dowel as an axle.

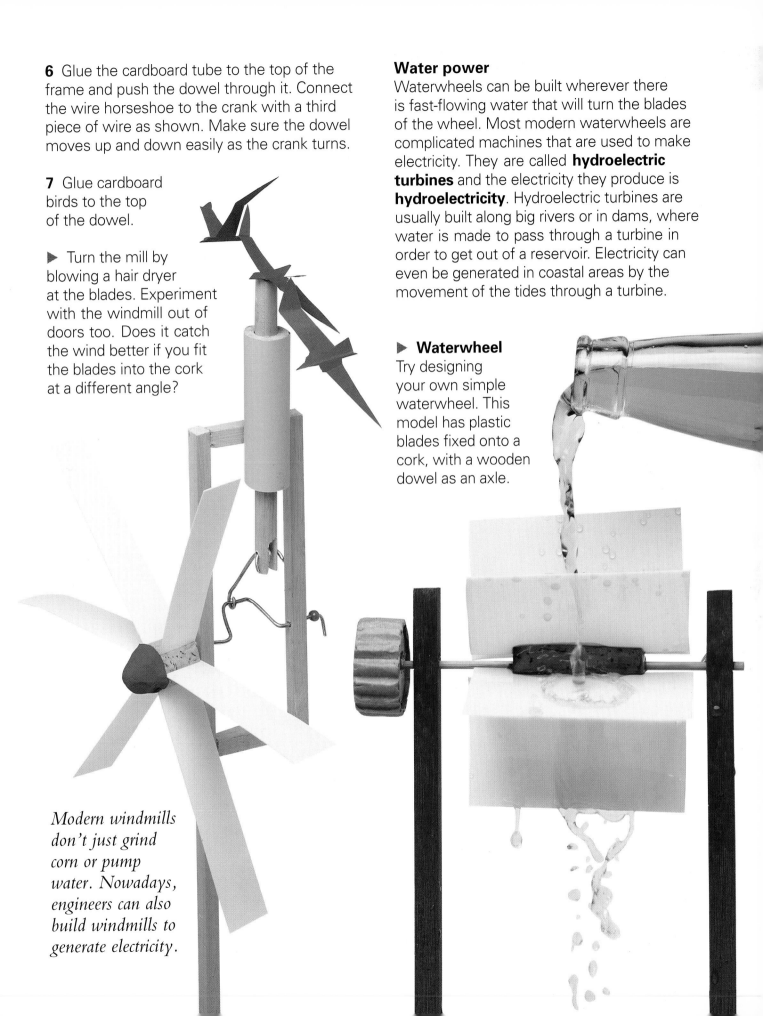

propeller

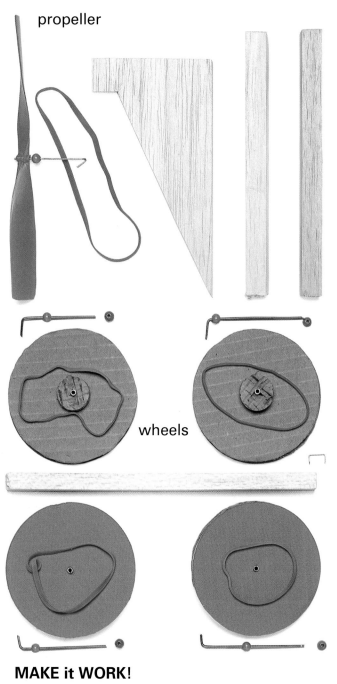

wheels

Rubber is an amazing material. You can stretch a rubber band to twice or three times its original length and it immediately springs back into shape when you let go. The stretched rubber stores energy. You can use this elastic energy to flick the band across the room, to make a catapult, or even to power model cars, boats, and planes.

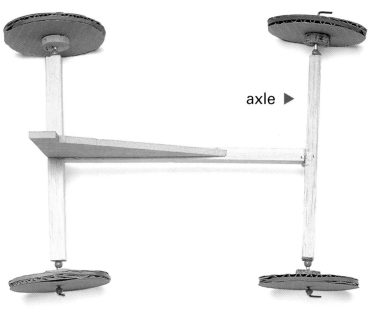

axle ▶

## MAKE it WORK!

This roadster uses energy stored in a twisted rubber band to turn a propeller. The propeller pushes against the air, driving the car forward.

## You will need

balsa wood
a thick needle
heavy cardboard
wire or thin nails
a plastic propeller
thick rubber bands
very short pieces of thin metal tubing

beads
a cork
a stapler
a paper clip
a craft knife

The roadster's cardboard wheels are difficult to make, so you might want to buy ready-made plastic wheels from a model shop.

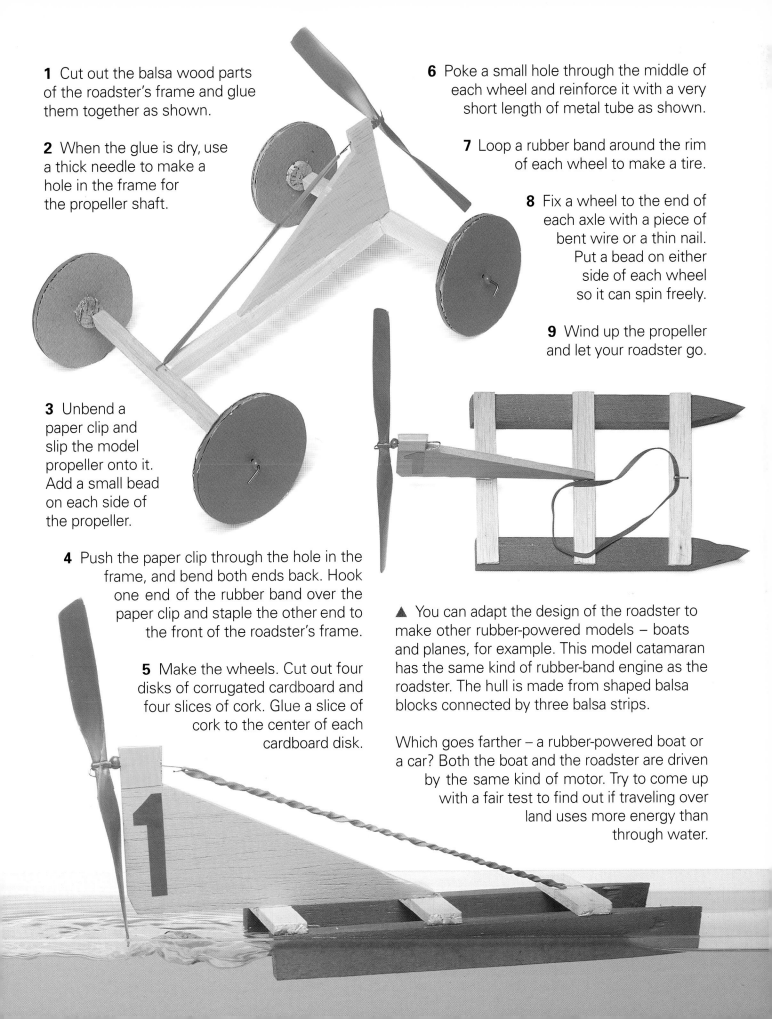

**1** Cut out the balsa wood parts of the roadster's frame and glue them together as shown.

**2** When the glue is dry, use a thick needle to make a hole in the frame for the propeller shaft.

**3** Unbend a paper clip and slip the model propeller onto it. Add a small bead on each side of the propeller.

**4** Push the paper clip through the hole in the frame, and bend both ends back. Hook one end of the rubber band over the paper clip and staple the other end to the front of the roadster's frame.

**5** Make the wheels. Cut out four disks of corrugated cardboard and four slices of cork. Glue a slice of cork to the center of each cardboard disk.

**6** Poke a small hole through the middle of each wheel and reinforce it with a very short length of metal tube as shown.

**7** Loop a rubber band around the rim of each wheel to make a tire.

**8** Fix a wheel to the end of each axle with a piece of bent wire or a thin nail. Put a bead on either side of each wheel so it can spin freely.

**9** Wind up the propeller and let your roadster go.

▲ You can adapt the design of the roadster to make other rubber-powered models – boats and planes, for example. This model catamaran has the same kind of rubber-band engine as the roadster. The hull is made from shaped balsa blocks connected by three balsa strips.

Which goes farther – a rubber-powered boat or a car? Both the boat and the roadster are driven by the same kind of motor. Try to come up with a fair test to find out if traveling over land uses more energy than through water.

For centuries, engineers dreamed of making machines that could fly like birds, but they didn't succeed until less than a hundred years ago. Because the force of gravity is so strong and air is so thin, a plane cannot get up off the ground unless it has a powerful engine and is very light for its size. A steam-powered plane carrying sacks of coal would never fly.

## You will need

a drill or awl
a plastic propeller
thin cardboard and balsa wood
two paper clips and a bead

strong glue
a craft knife
a rubber band
wire and a cork

**1** Cut the wing, tail plane, and rudder from cardboard.

**2** Make the fuselage. Cut two strips of balsa wood 10 inches long and two strips 2 inches long. Glue them together as shown.

**3** Use a thin drill or awl to make a small hole through each end of the fuselage.

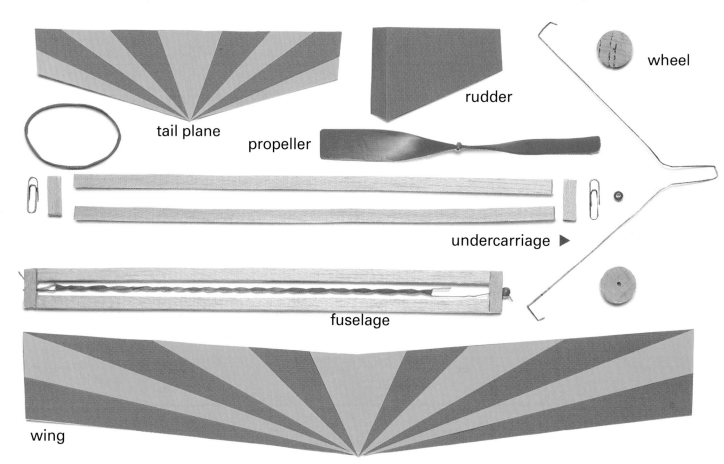

tail plane

rudder

wheel

propeller

undercarriage ▶

fuselage

wing

## MAKE it WORK!

Rubber is light, so it makes a good engine for a model plane. This model stays in the air for just a few seconds, but you'll find it travels farther than the roadster or the boat. Pushing through air is much easier than moving through water or rolling across the ground – so air travel can be more **efficient** than going by land or sea.

**4** Make two hooks out of paper clips. Loop the rubber band over them and fit one hook in each hole in the fuselage as shown.

**5** At the tail end, bend the hook all the way around and tape it firmly so that it won't move. At the propeller end, add a bead, so that the hook can spin freely.

**6** Attach the propeller and bend the paper clip hook around to hold it in place.

**7** Glue the wings, tail plane, and rudder in place.

**8** Bend the wire to make the undercarriage shape and push on slices of cork to make wheels. Glue the wire onto the fuselage.

**9** The plane is now complete – but before its first flight you must make sure that it balances well. Rest the wing tips on your fingers. If it does not balance, add small pieces of modeling clay to the nose or the tail until it is level.

**Test flight**
Wind up the propeller until the band is twisted tightly. Hold the plane just behind the wing and launch it gently into the air.

If your plane nose dives, add more weight to the tail. If the plane stalls (the nose tips up and the plane slows down) add more weight to the nose.

*Compared to gasoline, rubber doesn't store much energy, so a rubber-band motor only powers short flights. But in 1979 one model flew for over 52 minutes – a world record!*

When water boils, it changes into steam. The steam needs more space than the water, so it pushes against the things around it. The inventor of the first steam engine probably saw steam pushing the lid up off a boiling kettle and realized that this power could be used to push pistons and turn wheels.

## MAKE it WORK!

These model steamboats are powered by a candle. The candle's flame boils water inside a thin metal tube. Puffs of steam squirt from one end of the tube and push the boat along. More cold water is then sucked back into the tube, to replace the steam that has been puffed out.

## ▲ Bending the metal tube

To make a steamboat, you will need to twist a piece of brass or copper tubing. The easiest way to bend the tube is by winding it around a length of dowel. Make the bends slowly, taking care not to make kinks in the tube.

### You will need

a toothpick
a small candle
cardboard and glue
balsa wood
a wooden dowel
a piece of soft brass or copper tubing
a length of flexible plastic pipe that will
  fit neatly over the metal tubing

**1** Cut the balsa wood into the boat shape.

**2** Twist the metal tube as shown above.

**3** Ask an adult to help you push the two ends of metal tube through the balsa wood.

**4** Cut the flag, windshield, and number plate out of cardboard, and fold and glue them in place. Then glue the candle on the boat as shown.

**5** Push the plastic pipe over one end of the metal tube, and float the boat on the water.

**6** Suck some water into the metal tube through the plastic pipe. When the tube is full, pull off the plastic tube, taking care not to lift the boat out of the water. Light the candle and watch your boat go!

*The first steam engines did work that used to be done by horses, so an engine's strength was measured in horsepower. A 10-horsepower engine could do the work of ten horses. Today, even a small car engine has more than 50 horsepower. But our steamboat has only the power of a small insect!*

**▼ Steamboat race**
You could hold a race between two steamboats along lengths of plastic gutter that are filled with water.

What would you call a machine that repeats the same movement, hour after hour? It's a clock! A clock moves in a very regular way, counting out the passing minutes as it goes.

**MAKE it WORK!**

Building a clock isn't easy – most machines tend to slow down or to get faster as they work. A machine that works steadily needs careful engineering to control the speed. Try it for yourself with this marble-operated clock!

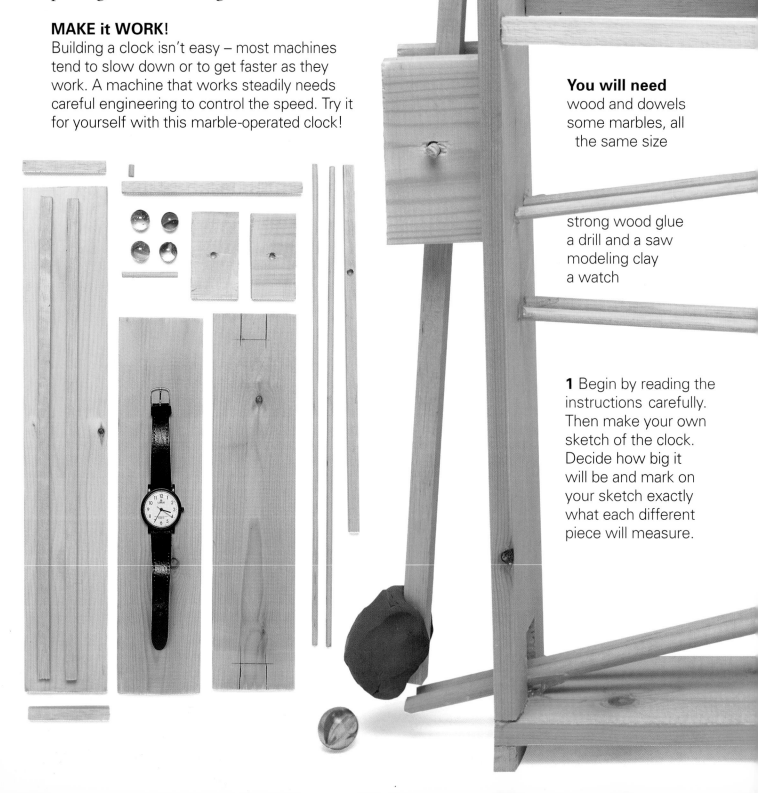

**You will need**
wood and dowels
some marbles, all
 the same size

strong wood glue
a drill and a saw
modeling clay
a watch

**1** Begin by reading the instructions carefully. Then make your own sketch of the clock. Decide how big it will be and mark on your sketch exactly what each different piece will measure.

**2** Ask an adult to help you cut the pieces of wood needed to make the clock's frame. Cut a slot at the top and bottom of one side piece in the positions shown.

**6** Cut two pieces of wood to make the lever arm. Drill a hole a third of the way down the longer piece. Glue both pieces together as shown, adding a small wooden stop to the end of the shorter piece.

**3** Firmly glue together the base, the side pieces, and the two top crossbars.

**7** Drill a hole in each of the lever supports and glue them to the frame. Fit the lever using a short dowel peg. Make sure the arm can swing freely.

**4** Cut eight lengths of dowel to make slopes for the marbles to run down. Measure the dowels carefully, so that they are all slightly longer than the crossbars.

**8** Start a marble on the run. At the bottom, it should knock the lever just hard enough to release the next marble.

**5** Glue the slopes in place. Adjust them carefully, so that the gap between the two dowels is smaller at the top end and gets wider farther down. At the bottom of each slope, the gap should be just wide enough for the marble to drop through and onto the slope below.

Use a watch with a second hand to time how long each marble takes to run from top to bottom.

**Adjusting the lever**
You'll probably need to adjust the lever to get it to work well. If more than one marble is released at once, add a modeling clay weight to the bottom of the lever.

A modern electronic clock is very accurate and reliable. It will run for over a year on just one tiny battery and will lose or gain no more than a few seconds in that time. Early clocks were much cruder.

All the clocks on this page have been used in the past. How accurate do you think they are? Try making them and test them against your own watch.

## Sand clocks

We still use sand clocks – sand running through an egg timer measures the minutes needed to cook a perfect boiled egg.

Make a cardboard funnel and fit it into the neck of a bottle. Fill the funnel with dry sand and see how long it takes to run through.

▶ Using a watch, make a scale on the sand clock. Mark the level of the sand at regular intervals (for example, every ten seconds). Are all of the marks evenly spaced? If not, why do you think the spacing changes?

## Candle clocks

Monks in the Middle Ages often used candles to measure the time. With the help of an adult, test a candle yourself to see how far it burns in an hour. Make hour marks along the rest of the candle with tape. Then mark the half and quarter hours too. How accurate is this clock?

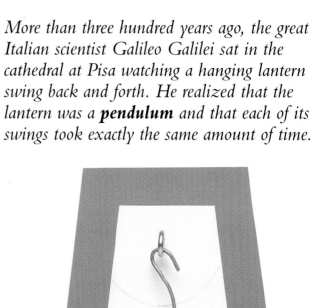

## Water clocks

Do you ever lie awake at night listening to a dripping faucet? The drips are sometimes so regular you can guess exactly when the next one is coming. The ancient Chinese used dripping water to invent elaborate water clocks.

## To make a water clock you will need

tape
a glass
a straw
modeling clay
a large wooden bead
an old plastic container

**1** Make a scale by marking the straw with tape. Attach the straw to the base of the glass with modeling clay.

**2** Slip the bead over the straw.

**3** Make a small hole in the bottom of the container. Then fill up the container with water and hold it over the glass.

**4** As water drips into the glass, the bead rises up the scale. If the water runs too slowly, make a larger hole. If it is too quick, tape over the hole to make it smaller.

*More than three hundred years ago, the great Italian scientist Galileo Galilei sat in the cathedral at Pisa watching a hanging lantern swing back and forth. He realized that the lantern was a **pendulum** and that each of its swings took exactly the same amount of time.*

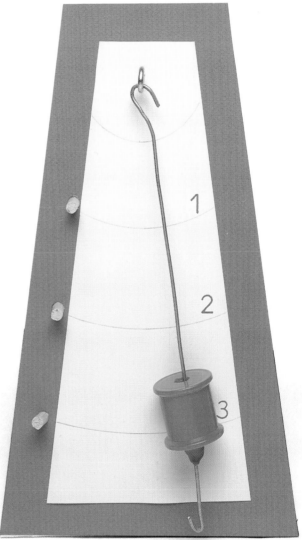

## ▲ Pendulum clock

A swinging pendulum is a good way of marking time. You can make a pendulum with a thread spool, modeling clay, and wire. Hang the spool from a hook and use your watch to investigate how the time taken by each swing changes as you move the spool up and down the wire.

Can you design any other machines of your own for measuring time?

# Electricity

Scientists study the universe and how it works. They ask themselves questions and then work out step-by-step methods to find the answers. Scientists start out with a **hypothesis**, a guess based on known facts. Then they test their idea by doing **experiments**, carefully observing and recording the results.

Investigating electricity is part of the science of **physics**. Physicists study **energy** and **matter** and try to make natural forces work for people. For instance, physicists discovered how to make **hydroelectric** and **atomic** power.

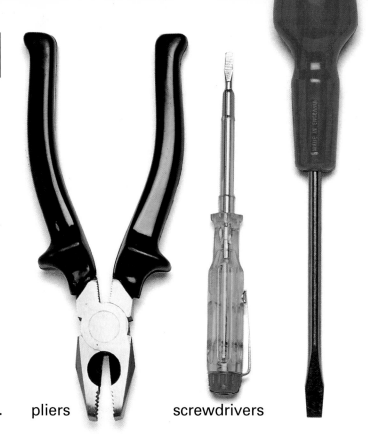

pliers          screwdrivers

## MAKE it WORK!

As you do the projects in this book, you will be investigating electricity and the science of physics for yourself. To understand how real scientists work, always use scientific methods. Draw detailed pictures or take photographs of your results, and write down clearly what you have done and observed.

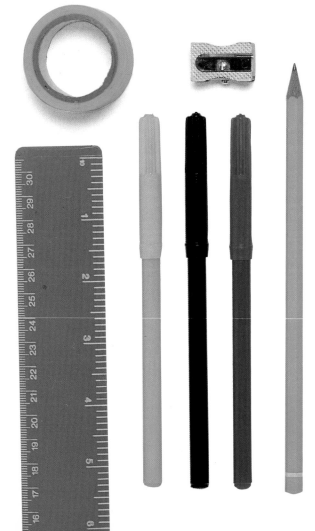

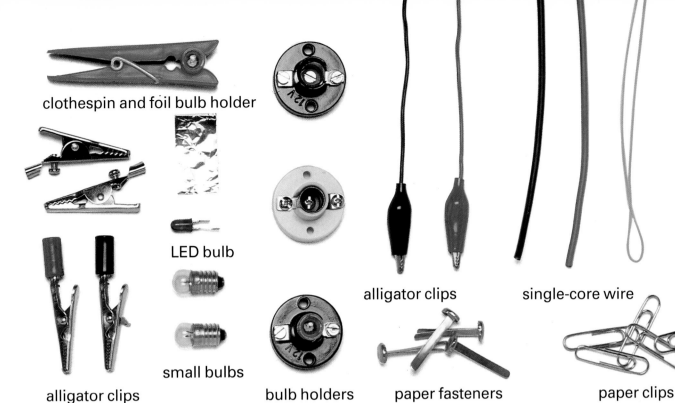

clothespin and foil bulb holder

LED bulb

small bulbs

alligator clips

bulb holders

alligator clips

single-core wire

paper fasteners

paper clips

electric motors

### You will need
Notebooks, pens, pencils, cardboard, poster board, tape, a plastic ruler, scissors, and a protractor. Other equipment can be found in hardware and art supply stores.

**Wire cutters** and **pliers**  Special wire cutters are best. You can use an old pair of scissors, but the wire will make them blunt.

**Screwdrivers**  You will need a small electrician's screwdriver with an insulated handle, as well as a larger one to screw pieces of wood together.

**Bulbs and bulb holders**  Use 6-volt bulbs and matching bulb holders. To make your own bulb holder, wrap aluminum foil around the base of a bulb and hold it in place with a clothespin.

**Wire**  Use single-core, plastic-coated wire.

**Clips**  Alligator clips are found in electrical goods stores, but metal paper clips or paper fasteners are inexpensive substitutes.

**Small electric motors**  Use 3-volt or 6-volt motors from a hobby shop.

**Buzzers** and **magnets**  These are sold in model shops and hardware stores.

**Batteries**  Most of the activities in this book use simple 6-volt batteries.

**Be careful!**  Never touch car batteries and never plug anything into the sockets in your home. Household electricity and large batteries are extremely dangerous!

horseshoe magnet

6-volt battery

When you comb your hair, does it sometimes stand straight up and stick to the comb? That's **static electricity**.

All things are made up of tiny particles called **atoms**. When a comb and hair rub together, the outer layers of **electrons** are rubbed off the hair atoms and cling to the atoms of the comb, producing static electricity.

When atoms lose electrons, we say they become positively charged. When they gain electrons, they are negatively charged. Two like charges repel one another—and different charges, like the hair and the comb, attract each other.

### Repelling
Rub two balloons against your sweater and tie them to a stick with the rubbed sides facing each other. Because both balloons have the same charge, they swing away from one another.

**MAKE it WORK!**
With an **electroscope** you can test for the presence and strength of static electricity.

**You will need**

| | |
|---|---|
| a glass jar with a plastic lid | bare wire |
| foil from a candy wrapper | aluminum foil |
| plastic pen or ruler | piece of silk or wool |

Ask an adult to help you push a piece of wire through the lid of a jar. Bend one end of the wire and drape a thin piece of foil from a candy wrapper over it. Crumple a ball of aluminum foil around the other end. Rub a plastic pen with a piece of silk or wool, then hold it over the foil ball. If the pen is charged, the candy wrapper will move. Try rubbing some other objects and see what happens.

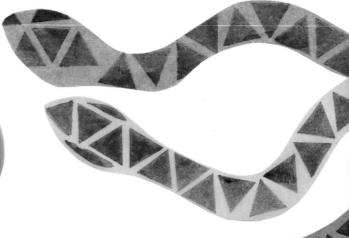

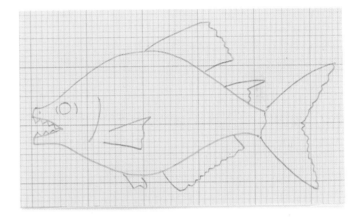

## Attracting

Make some piranhas like the ones above. Using the graph paper shape at right as a pattern, cut out fish from a single layer of colored tissue paper. Place them on a flat surface. Rub a plastic ruler with a piece of silk or wool to get the ruler's electrons moving. Now pass the ruler over the fish and watch them jump up, attracted by the electric charge.

▼ Make some curly tissue-paper snakes and decorate them using stencils or felt-tip pens. (Be careful because tissue paper tears easily.) Pass a charged ruler over them—and watch them wiggle and wriggle!

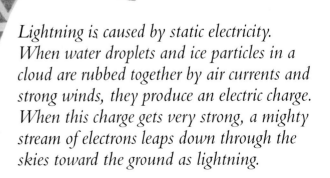

*Lightning is caused by static electricity. When water droplets and ice particles in a cloud are rubbed together by air currents and strong winds, they produce an electric charge. When this charge gets very strong, a mighty stream of electrons leaps down through the skies toward the ground as lightning.*

Static electricity itself isn't very useful to us—we have to harness electricity before it can be used. The power that we actually use in our homes is called **current electricity** and is made up of millions of moving electrons.

An electric current is formed when the electrons in a substance, such as a piece of wire, are all made to move in the same direction. To provide us with electrical energy, the electrons must flow in an uninterrupted loop, called an electrical **circuit**.

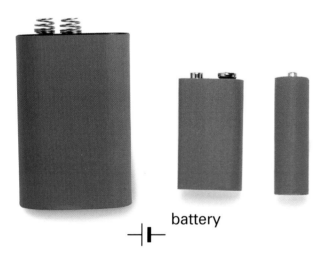

battery

▲ All the projects and activities in this book use small batteries as the source of power.

▲ Scientists and electrical engineers use special symbols when they are drawing a diagram of a circuit. This is the symbol for a bulb inside a bulb holder. Did you spot the symbol for a battery above?

bulbs        bulb holder

## MAKE it WORK!

Making a simple circuit is easy, but make sure that all your connections are properly made.

### You will need

6-volt battery                          bulb and
1 foot of plastic-coated wire    bulb holder
paper clips/alligator clips
pencil, key, cork, eraser, fork, and other
  household objects

**1** Cut the wire in half. Use wire cutters or pliers to strip the plastic coating from the ends, without cutting the wire itself.

**2** Wrap the bare end of one piece of wire around each connecting screw on your bulb holder. Tighten the screws to hold the wire in place.

**3** Attach the other ends of the wires to clips and attach the clips to the battery **terminals**. If all connections are made properly, the bulb will light.

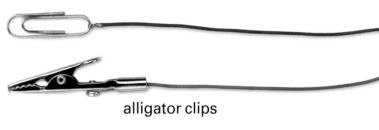

alligator clips

*Anything that an electric current can flow through, such as metal, is called a **conductor**. But materials such as plastic, rubber, and glass do not allow electricity to pass through them. These are called **insulators**. Electrical circuits use both conductors and insulators. The metal in the wire is a conductor that allows the current to flow throughout the circuit. The plastic around the wires and on the bulb holders is an insulator and stops the current from passing into any metal objects that the circuit may be touching.*

▶ All circuits are made up of three basic elements: the conductor (the wire); the **load**, which uses the electricity (in this case a bulb); and the energy source (the battery).

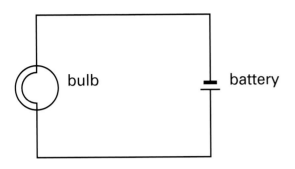

## Conductor test

Test some household objects to see if they are conductors or insulators. Make a simple circuit with a gap in it, like the one below right. Touch an object with both wires. If the bulb lights up, you know that electricity must be passing through in order to complete the circuit. That means that the object must be a conductor.

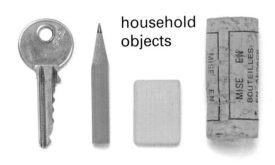

household objects

▶ Electrons flow through some materials better than others. The bulb shines brightly with a good conductor in the circuit and dimly with a poor one.

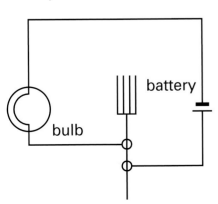

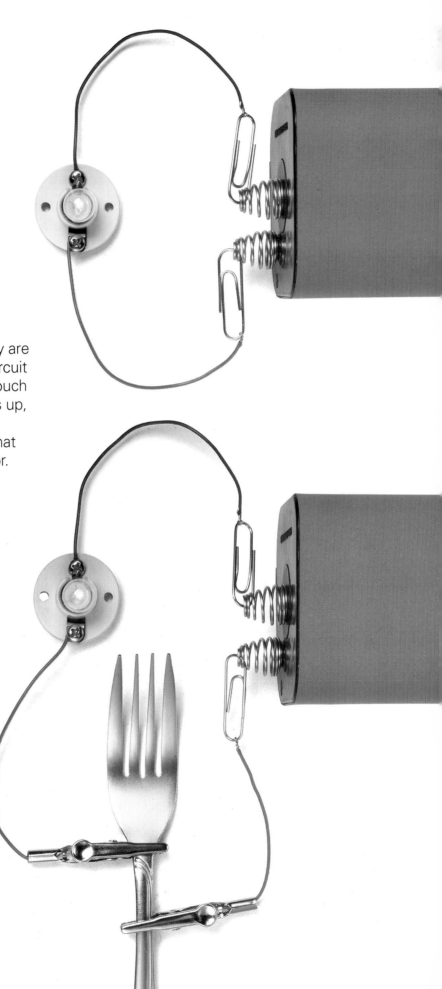

Batteries produce electricity from chemical energy. Usually, two metals, called electrodes, are placed in an **acid** solution called an **electrolyte**. A chemical reaction takes place and creates electric power.

## MAKE it WORK!

There are many kinds of batteries. Wet batteries have metal plates in liquid acid. Dry batteries have a chemical paste that separates a carbon rod from a zinc case. Other batteries use other metals and an **alkaline** substance to work.

### To make a wet battery you will need

| | |
|---|---|
| glass jar | white vinegar |
| wire | alligator clips or paper clips |
| strip of zinc | piece of copper pipe |
| light emitting-diode (LED) | |

**1** Put the strips of metal in the jar and fill it with vinegar. Vinegar is a kind of acid and will be the electrolyte in your battery.

**2** When you attach clips and wires as shown, the bulb will light up. However, LEDs work only when wired the right way. If yours doesn't light the first time, reverse the connections.

### Positive and negative

Our wet battery uses two metals, zinc and copper, to make a current. When these are put into acid, negative electrons move through the liquid from the copper to the zinc. From the zinc, they move down the wire, through the LED, and back up the wire to the copper, completing a circuit and causing an electric flow.

*The first battery was invented in the 1790s by an Italian nobleman, Alessandro Volta. It used disks of silver and zinc, just like our coin battery.*

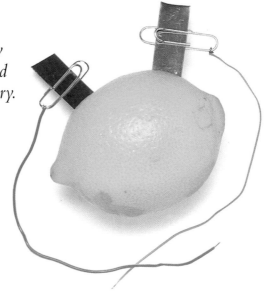

## To make a battery tester you will need

| | |
|---|---|
| balsa wood | cardboard |
| insulated copper wire | compass |
| 2 screws and washers | wire and clips |

**1** Secure the compass to the cardboard with copper wire. Attach the ends of the wire to screws on the wooden base.

**2** To test a battery, clip wires from the battery terminals to the screws. The compass needle will move. Try this with a brand-new battery, and one that has been used a lot. Can you notice a difference?

▲ **Minibatteries** You can make a coin battery using silver and copper coins. Separate a copper coin from a silver coin with several thicknesses of paper towel soaked in saltwater. With tape, attach wires to both coins. Don't let the wires touch each other, but clip them to your battery tester and see what happens. The current won't be very strong, but the tester should show some reaction.

You can also make a low-voltage minibattery by pushing copper and zinc strips into a lemon.

Electricity has many uses—in homes, factories, and schools. It is produced in power stations by burning coal or oil fuels to power electricity **generators**. It can also be produced from nuclear fuel or in hydroelectric turbines.

## MAKE it WORK!

Lighthouses were among the first users of electric power. Put your circuit-building know-how to good use and make a battery-operated minilighthouse for your bedroom.

### You will need

| | |
|---|---|
| thin cardboard | glue and tape |
| utility knife/scissors | wire |
| bulb and bulb holder | 6-volt battery |
| alligator clips/paper clips | toothpick |

**1** Make a round tube from a piece of white cardboard and decorate it with red stripes. You could also use the tube from a roll of toilet paper and cover it with white paper.

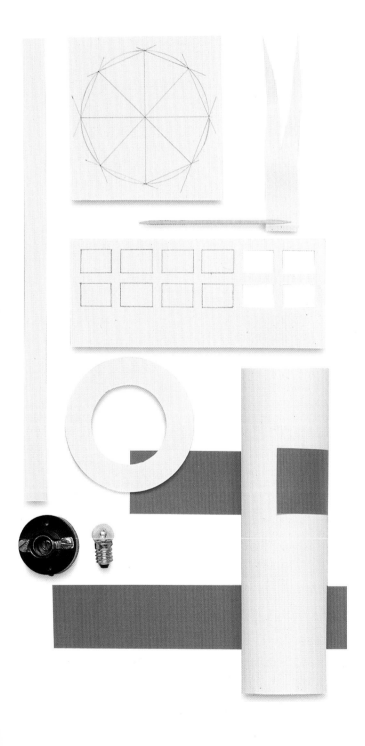

**2** To make the balcony, cut out a circle of cardboard, make a hole in the center, and glue or tape it to the top of the tube. Glue a strip of cardboard around the edge of the balcony to make the railing.

**3** Attach two long wires to a bulb holder and tape the bulb holder into place at the top of the tube. Push the wires down through the tube and out the bottom.

**4** Use a strip of cardboard to make the windows at the top of the lighthouse. Using the picture on the left as a guide, cut out small squares with scissors or ask an adult to use a utility knife. Then bend the cardboard to make a cylindrical shape and glue it in place on the balcony.

**5** To make the roof, draw a circle and make a cut from the rim to the center. Fold the circle to form a cone and glue it. Make a flag from paper and a toothpick.

**6** Attach the ends of the wires to a battery and the bulb in your lighthouse will light.

*Scientists measure electricity with two separate units called volts and watts. **Volts** measure electrical force, the amount of power produced by a source of electricity, such as a battery. **Watts** measure the electrical power at the point where it is actually used—in an electric heater or light bulb for instance.*

*The ancient Egyptians were probably the first people to build lighthouses. They began by lighting bonfires on hilltops to guide their ships. During the third century B.C., they built the tallest lighthouse ever, the Pharos of Alexandria, which was over 400 feet (122 meters) high!*

▲ To hide the battery, make a "rock" out of pieces of old cardboard, stuck together in a jagged shape and painted. Make a series of buoys like those on the next page to go around your lighthouse.

All the parts of an electrical circuit must be joined up to one another so that the current can flow. There are two basic ways to wire a circuit with more than one **component** (or part)—in series or in parallel.

## MAKE it WORK!

**In a series circuit**, the electric current flows along a single path, going through each component in turn. If one component is removed or breaks (when a Christmas-tree bulb burns out, for instance), all the other components will stop working, too.

**In a parallel circuit**, each component is connected to the power source on its own branch of the main circuit. Even if one of the bulbs in a parallel circuit burns out, the other bulbs will continue to shine because their own branches of the circuit remain complete.

## You will need

thin cardboard or construction paper
scissors/utility knife        glue and tape
batteries                           wire
bulbs and bulb holders
alligator clips/paper clips

**1** You are going to make a string of buoys like the ones used to mark shipping lanes. For each buoy you will need to cut out the shapes you see below from thin cardboard: a semicircle for the body, a strip with windows for the lantern, and a circle with a slit in it for the cone-shaped top. Ask an adult to cut out the windows with a utility knife.

**2** Assemble the buoys as shown below, taping a bulb holder firmly into the body of each buoy.

**3** Wire the series circuit as shown on the left-hand side of the opposite page. Run a wire from bulb holder to bulb holder, completing the circuit from the last buoy back to the battery.

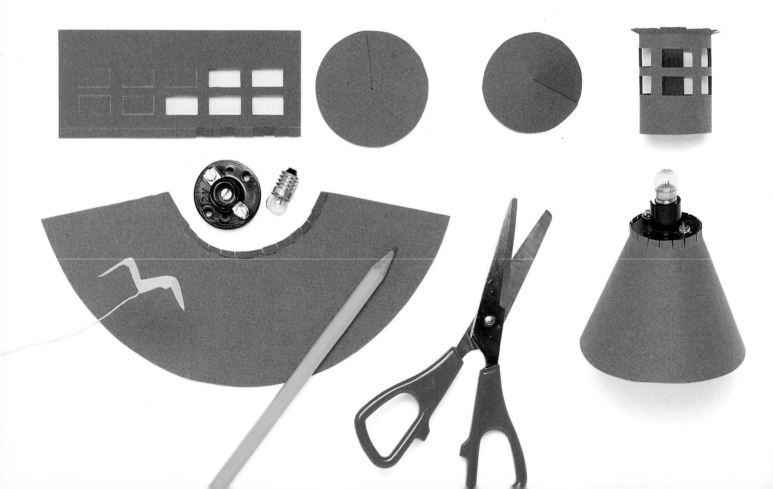

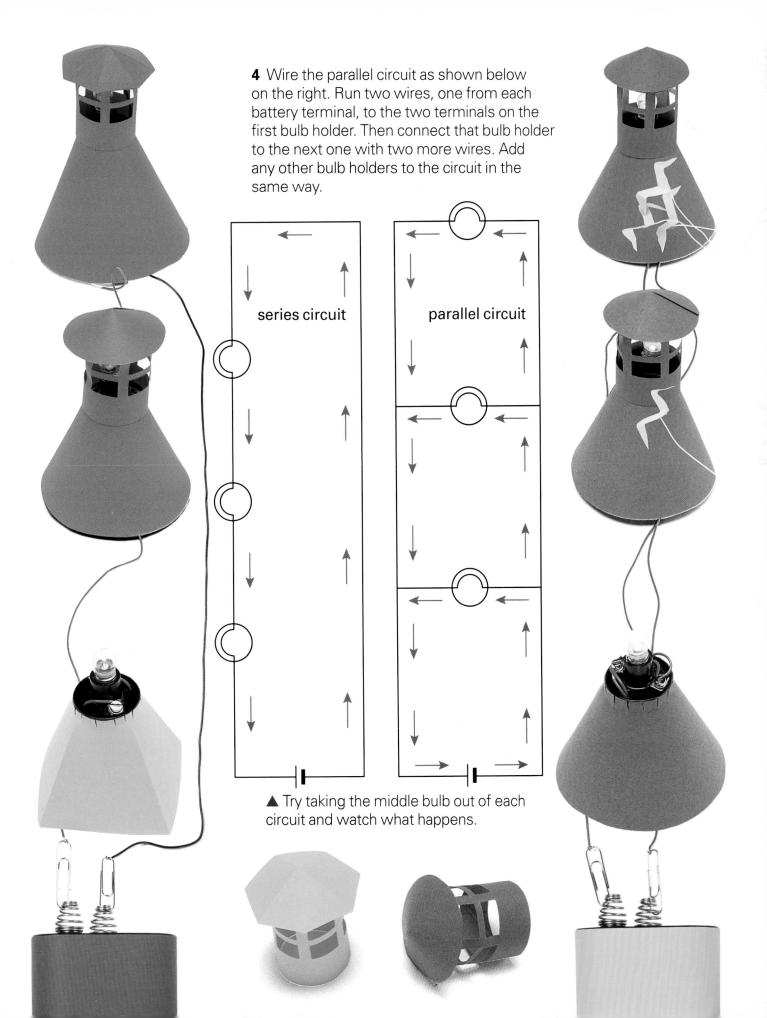

**4** Wire the parallel circuit as shown below on the right. Run two wires, one from each battery terminal, to the two terminals on the first bulb holder. Then connect that bulb holder to the next one with two more wires. Add any other bulb holders to the circuit in the same way.

series circuit

parallel circuit

▲ Try taking the middle bulb out of each circuit and watch what happens.

Light bulbs are used to produce light from electricity. Each bulb contains a thin metal thread called a **filament**. When an electric current forces its way through this thin part of the circuit, the filament glows a bright white color and the bulb gives off light.

**You will need**
old light bulbs
scissors
glue or tape
cardboard
ruler

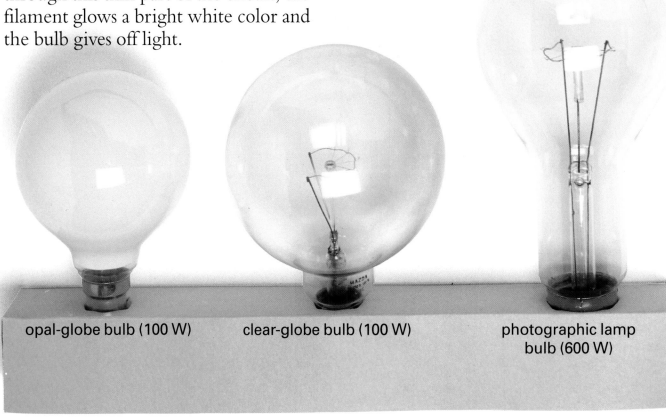

opal-globe bulb (100 W)     clear-globe bulb (100 W)     photographic lamp bulb (600 W)

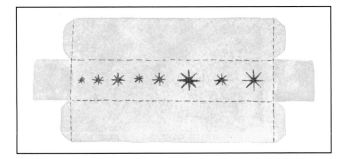

## MAKE it WORK!

Light bulbs come in all shapes and sizes. Collect different light bulbs and make a special box to display and store your collection. New bulbs are expensive, so just collect ones that have burned out. Always handle light bulbs carefully because the glass is very delicate.

**1** Decide what size you want your box to be. Then cut out a flat shape like the one on the left.

**2** Fold the cardboard up along the dotted lines. Tuck in the corner flaps and glue or tape them in place.

**3** Carefully cut star-shaped slits in the top of the box. Press the ends of the bulbs into the centers of the stars. Make sure that the bulbs fit firmly.

**4** Label your collection. Mark whether each bulb has a filament or a fluorescent tube and also how bright it is. You can tell the brightness of a bulb from the number of watts (W) of power that it uses.

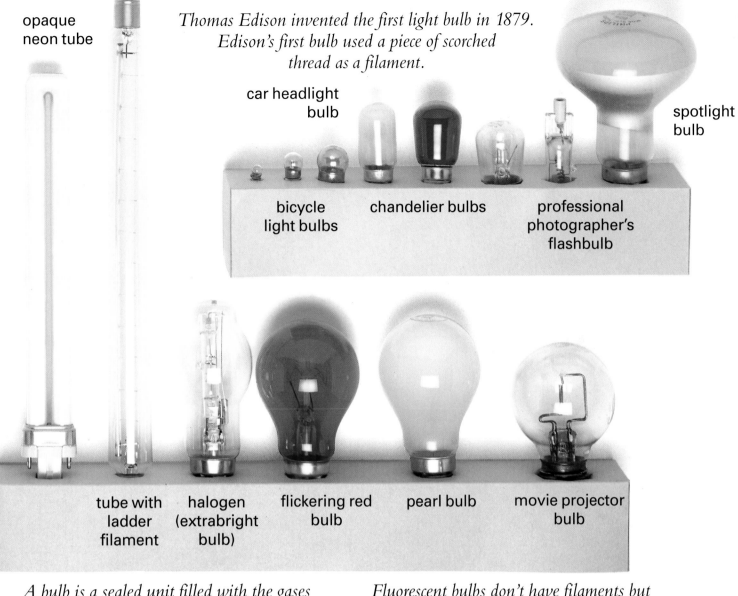

opaque neon tube

*Thomas Edison invented the first light bulb in 1879. Edison's first bulb used a piece of scorched thread as a filament.*

car headlight bulb

spotlight bulb

bicycle light bulbs

chandelier bulbs

professional photographer's flashbulb

tube with ladder filament

halogen (extrabright bulb)

flickering red bulb

pearl bulb

movie projector bulb

*A bulb is a sealed unit filled with the gases nitrogen or argon. It contains no oxygen, the gas in the air that substances need to burn. Nitrogen or argon lets the filament glow but doesn't allow it to catch fire.*

*Fluorescent bulbs don't have filaments but contain a gas under pressure. When electricity passes through the bulb, the gas gives off light, but the bulb stays cool.*

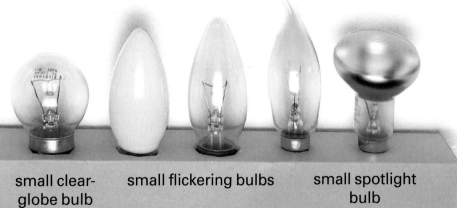

small clear-globe bulb

small flickering bulbs

small spotlight bulb

An electric current must always flow through a complete circuit. Current can't flow in a broken circuit because electrons have to keep moving in a continuous stream.

## MAKE it WORK!

How steady is your hand? Find out with this circuit game. At the start of the game, the circuit is broken, so the light is off. If your hand shakes as you move the playing stick along, the loop touches the wire, the circuit is completed, and the bulb lights up!

### You will need

| | |
|---|---|
| battery | wire |
| bulb and bulb holder | dowel |
| alligator clips/paper clips | colored tape |
| wire coat hanger | sandpaper |
| screw eyes, large and small | |
| balsa wood and wood glue, or shoe box | |

Some coat hangers are coated with a thin layer of clear plastic so they won't mark your clothes. Remove the plastic with a piece of sandpaper—otherwise the plastic will insulate the wire and the circuit won't work.

**1** Make the playing stick by screwing a large screw eye into the end of the dowel. Wrap one end of a long piece of stripped wire around the base of the eye. Tape the wire along the dowel. Some wire should be left hanging at the end.

**2** Make a box by gluing together pieces of wood, or use a shoe box. Paint the box, then divide into sections with colored tape.

**3** Position the bulb holder at one end of the box, wire it, and push the wires through the top of the box.

screw eye          dowel

wire

**4** Twist a small screw eye into each end of the box. If you are using a shoe box, you may have to tape them in place. Bend and twist the coat hanger wire to make the top part of the game. Thread the bent wire through the screw eye in the playing stick. Then connect the ends of the coat hanger wire to the screw eyes on the box.

**5** Beneath the box, connect one of the wires from the bulb holder to the battery. Put an alligator clip on the other bulb holder wire and attach it to one end of the bent coat hanger.

**6** Connect the wire from the playing stick to the free battery terminal. Now you're ready to play!

### circuit diagram of the circuit game

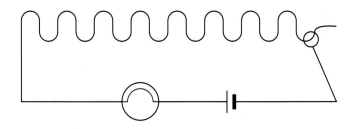

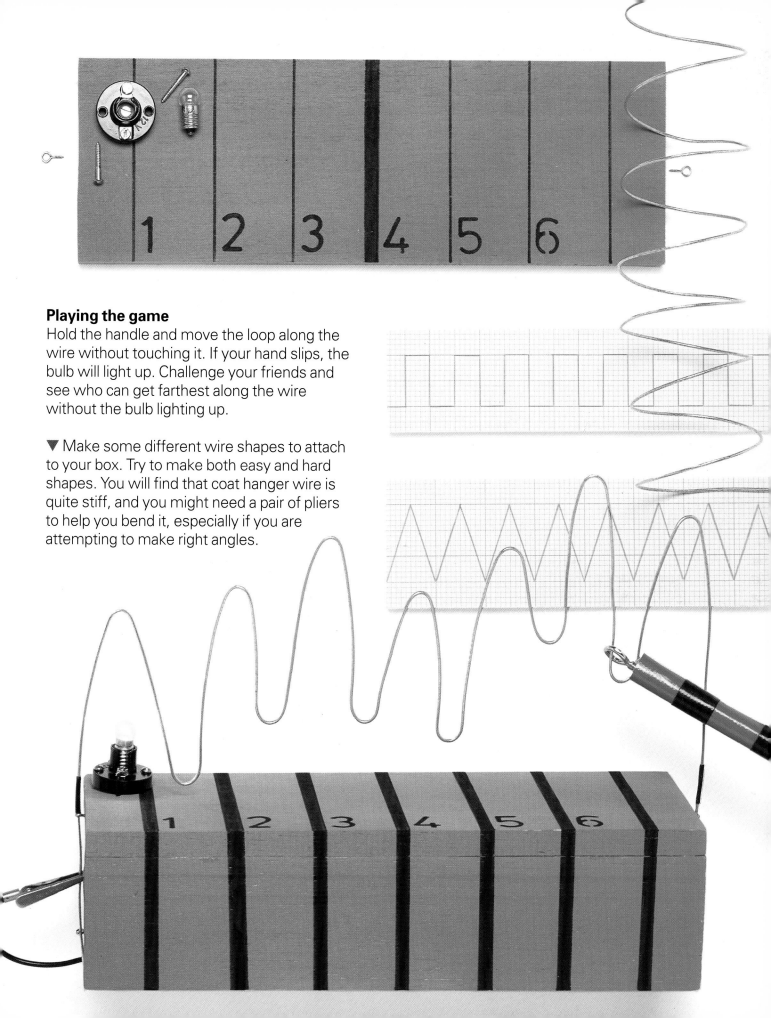

## Playing the game

Hold the handle and move the loop along the wire without touching it. If your hand slips, the bulb will light up. Challenge your friends and see who can get farthest along the wire without the bulb lighting up.

▼ Make some different wire shapes to attach to your box. Try to make both easy and hard shapes. You will find that coat hanger wire is quite stiff, and you might need a pair of pliers to help you bend it, especially if you are attempting to make right angles.

Switches are used to turn electrical circuits on and off. When they are switched off, they break the circuit so that electricity can't flow around it. When they are switched on, they complete the circuit, allowing the electricity to flow through.

## MAKE it WORK!

Switches can be made to work in lots of different ways. For instance, you may not want a light to go out completely but just to be a little less bright. Or you may need a switch that can turn a buzzer on and off very quickly to make a special pattern of signals. Here are four different types of switches for you to try.

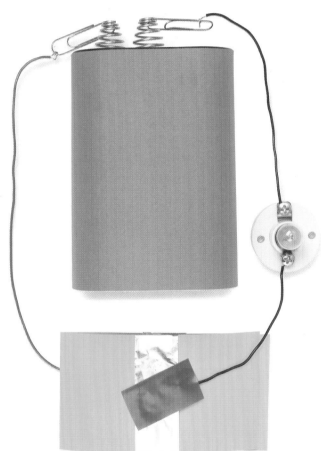

### Simple switch

This is a simple on/off switch. When it is on, the current flows through the circuit; when it is off, the current stops. Wire a simple circuit, like the one on pages 54-55, but leave a break in the wires. Make a switch as shown above, using a block of balsa wood, a paper clip and two metal thumbtacks. When the clip touches both thumbtacks, the switch is on.

### Pressure switch

This type of switch can be used to make a doorbell ring when someone steps on a doormat. Wire a circuit as before. Fold a piece of cardboard in half. Wrap strips of foil around each half of the cardboard, so that they touch when pressed together. Tape the wires to the foil on the outside of each side of the cardboard. When the two strips of foil touch, the switch is on.

◀ These are low-voltage switches from a model shop. You can include them in any of the circuits shown in this book.

## You will need

| | |
|---|---|
| 6-volt batteries | cork |
| bulb holders | wire |
| balsa wood | tape |
| paper clips | bulbs |
| thumbtacks | pencil |
| aluminum foil | cardboard |
| thin copper strips | utility knife |
| | alligator clips |

## Dimmer switch

Electricity can pass through the **graphite** in a pencil, but it is hard work. Graphite is called a **resistor**, because it offers resistance to the electric current. You can use a graphite pencil resistor to make a dimmer switch. The longer your pencil lead, the more resistance there is and the dimmer your light will be.

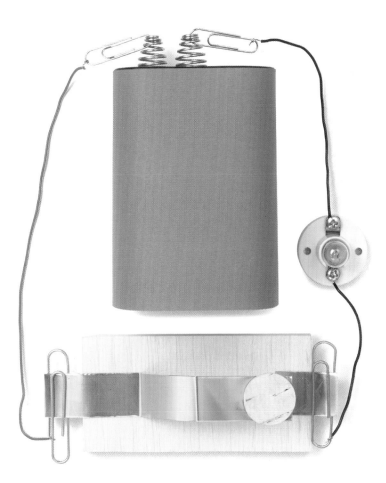

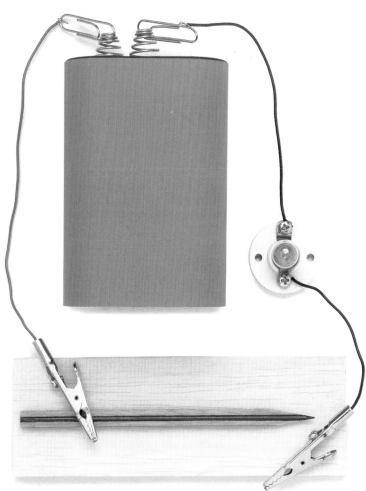

## Tapper switch

This switch is used by Morse code operators. It gives the operator total control over the length of time the circuit is complete or broken. The switch is on when the two strips of copper are pressed together. It returns automatically to the "off" position when not in use. The full instructions for how to make a Morse code tapper are given on the next page.

Make a simple circuit as before, but fit alligator clips to the free ends of the wire. Soak a pencil in water, and then ask an adult to slice it open down the middle with a utility knife. (**Be careful!** Do not try to cut the pencil yourself.) Attach the alligator clips to opposite ends of the pencil lead; gradually slide one clip toward the other. What happens?

Morse code was invented in 1840 by Samuel Morse, an American inventor and painter. Each letter of the alphabet is represented by a simple combination of long and short electrical signals that can easily be transmitted down a single wire. The code is written as dots, dashes, and spaces. Before the days of satellites and fax machines, all international newspaper reports and messages were sent flashing and buzzing down telegraph wires by Morse code operators.

## MAKE it WORK!
Make your own Morse code tappers to send and receive secret messages.

### You will need
| | |
|---|---|
| 2 pieces of wood | 2 batteries |
| 2 bulbs and bulb holders | wire |
| 2 strips of copper | paper clips |
| 2 slices of cork | glue and screws |
| hacksaw (and an adult to use it) | |

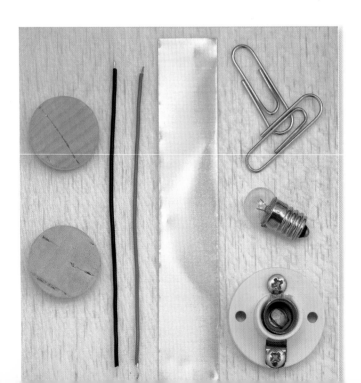

## ▼ International Morse code
These are the Morse code symbols. As you can see, they are made up of dots, dashes, and spaces. A dot is transmitted by pressing and instantly releasing the transmitter key. To send a dash, hold the key down twice as long as you did for the dot. A space between letters is the same length as a dot, and a space between words is the same length as a dash.

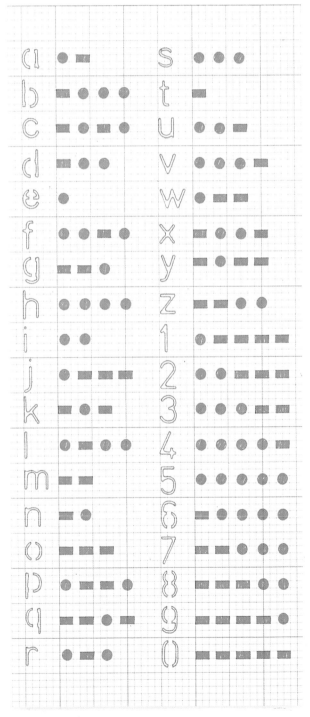

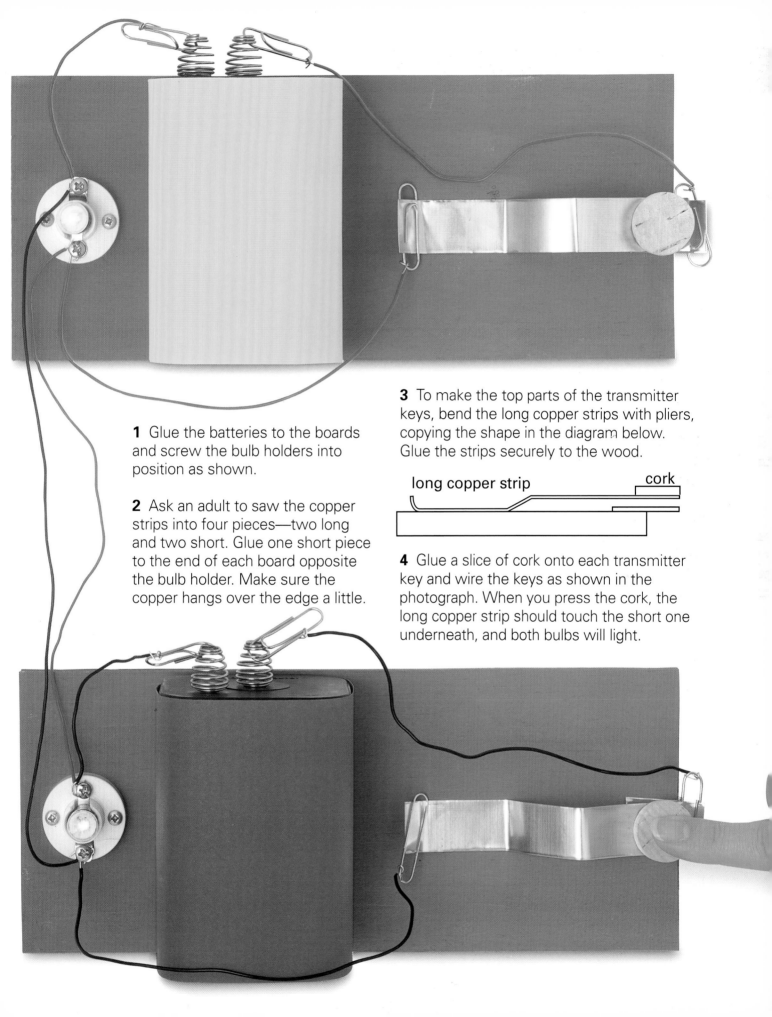

**1** Glue the batteries to the boards and screw the bulb holders into position as shown.

**2** Ask an adult to saw the copper strips into four pieces—two long and two short. Glue one short piece to the end of each board opposite the bulb holder. Make sure the copper hangs over the edge a little.

**3** To make the top parts of the transmitter keys, bend the long copper strips with pliers, copying the shape in the diagram below. Glue the strips securely to the wood.

long copper strip      cork

**4** Glue a slice of cork onto each transmitter key and wire the keys as shown in the photograph. When you press the cork, the long copper strip should touch the short one underneath, and both bulbs will light.

Some circuits are made up of lots of different connections that act together to perform complex tasks. Electrical equipment, such as radios, uses many tiny circuits, and the circuits themselves may not be made of wire but tiny strips of metal printed on a sheet. In computers, thousands of microscopic circuits are crammed onto one **silicon chip**.

## MAKE it WORK!

Most circuits are made on a circuit board. The wires are spaced out so they cannot accidentally touch one another. This question-and-answer game shows you what a simple circuit board looks like. Each connection, when correctly made, will complete a circuit, and the bulb will light up.

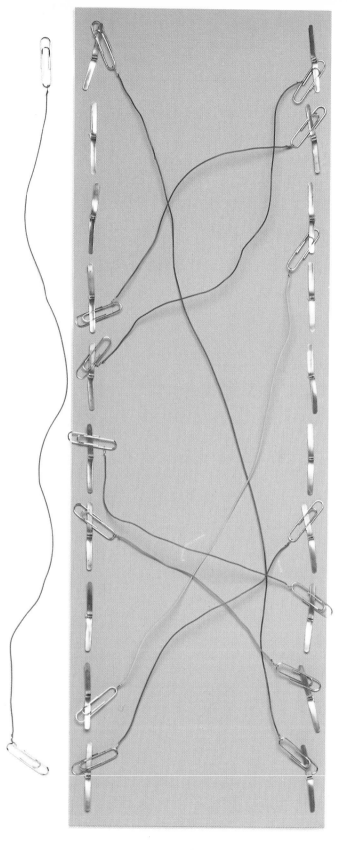

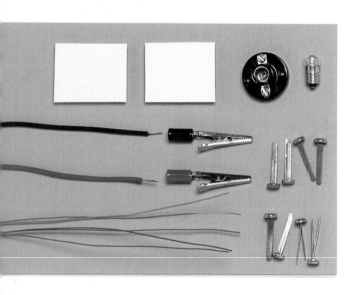

### You will need

wire and battery
bulb and bulb holder
alligator/paper clips
stick-on hook-and-
   loop fasteners

stiff cardboard
paper fasteners
colored pens
magazine pictures
buzzer

**1** Cut a piece of cardboard for your quiz board. Push in paper fasteners along each side of the cardboard. On the front of the cardboard, stick strips of hook-and-loop fasteners next to each paper fastener.

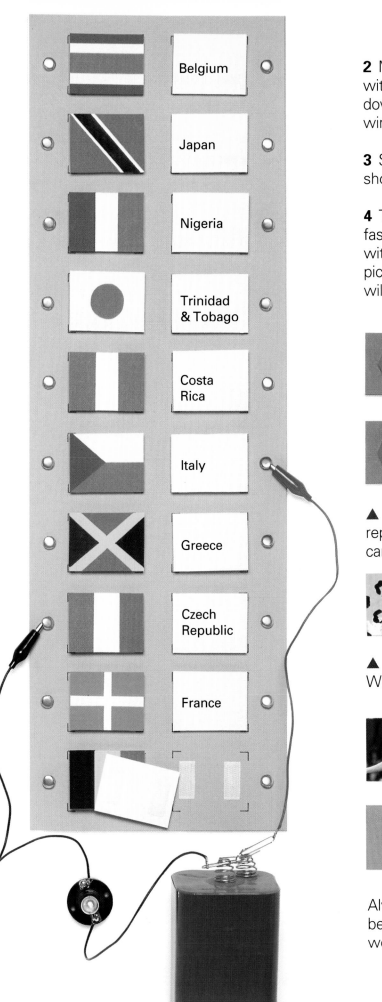

Belgium

Japan

Nigeria

Trinidad & Tobago

Costa Rica

Italy

Greece

Czech Republic

France

**2** Make question and answer cards. Back them with hook-and-loop fasteners and stick them down in random order. On the back of the board, wire each question to its correct answer.

**3** Set up the battery, bulb, wires, and clips as shown.

**4** Touch a testing wire to one of the paper fasteners on the question side. Then match it up with an answer on the other side. If you have picked the correct answer, the electrical circuit will be completed and the bulb will light up.

▲ Make raised shapes for your quiz board and replace the light bulb with a buzzer. Now you can play blindfolded!

▲ ▼ Think up different quizzes for your board. What about animals, or tennis players?

 Graf  McEnroe  Lendl

Always check your connections carefully before you start to play. The game will not work if any of the wires become loose.

Like static electricity, **magnetism** is a natural, invisible force that makes certain objects attract or repel one another. The ancient Greeks noticed that certain rocks were magnets. Today we know that magnets work because of the motion of electric charges.

### What is a magnet?

A magnet is a piece of iron or steel that attracts or repels certain other pieces of iron or steel. Like all substances, metals are made up of tiny particles called **molecules**, which in turn are made up of atoms. Normally, all the molecules in a piece of iron are facing in different directions. However, if we can rearrange the molecules so that they all face the same way, they will act together as a magnet, making a powerful force.

## MAKE it WORK!

You can watch the power of magnets at work with this fishing game. The object is to catch as many high-scoring fish as possible. Players take turns fishing, and the winner is the player with the highest score.

**1** Cut out large, medium, and small fish shapes from different colors of cardboard.

**2** Draw in the eye, gills, and mouth with a black marker.

**3** To get a fish-scale effect, tap paint onto the fish using a stencil brush and a piece of wire mesh. Use a lighter-colored paint for the belly. When the paint has dried, write a score number on each fish.

**You will need**
a small magnet with a hole in the center
thin cardboard          paint
black marker            utility knife
dowel and string        thin wire mesh
paper clips             stencil brushes

**4** Make a fishing line by tying the magnet to the string. Attach the other end of the string to the dowel rod.

**5** Attach a paper clip to each fish's mouth.

**6** Make a sea from a cardboard box painted blue. Put in the fish and start fishing!

Around a magnet is an area called a **force field**, where the pull or push of metal and magnet is at its strongest. The force field may be strong enough to pass through wood or glass. The ends of a magnet, where most of the energy is directed, are much more powerful than the middle.

## MAKE it WORK

The more powerful the magnet, the larger and stronger its force field. See how a small magnet works through cardboard and how the force field of a strong steel magnet can pass through a wooden door.

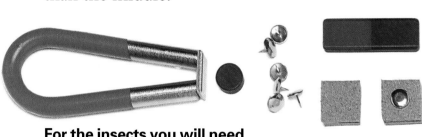

### For the insects you will need

| | |
|---|---|
| cardboard | glue |
| slices of cork | paint and paintbrushes |
| metal thumbtacks | horseshoe magnet |
| utility knife/ scissors | |

## Magnetic insects

Ask an adult to cut out insect shapes from cardboard with a utility knife. Paint the shapes and glue each one onto a small square of cork. Push a thumbtack into the other side of the cork. From the other side of a door, use a strong horseshoe magnet to make the insects move.

## For the soccer game you will need

| | |
|---|---|
| white cardboard | green cardboard |
| utility knife | cork |
| metal thumbtacks | dowels |
| small magnets | glue |
| tiny ball | paints or crayons |

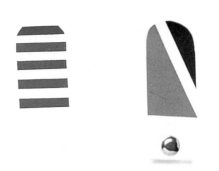

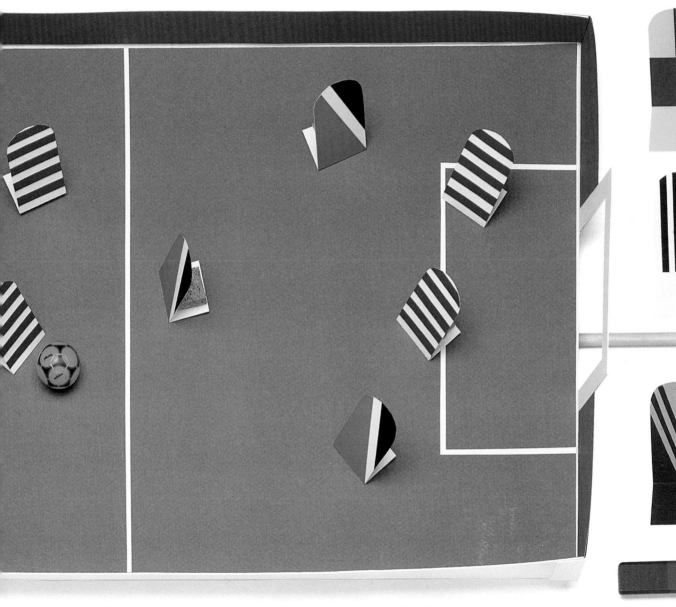

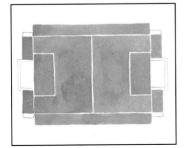

## Table soccer

Make a box out of green cardboard, folding and gluing the corners as shown. Draw the lines of the soccer field in white. Make cardboard players with a piece of cork glued to the inside of each base. Stick a thumbtack through from the outside. The players are moved from under the box by magnets attached to dowels.

The force fields of magnets can pass through many different substances. The magnetic insects and magnetic soccer on the previous pages work because magnets can attract through wood and cardboard. A magnetic force field can also pass through water.

## You will need

| | |
|---|---|
| colored poster board | wire |
| corks | paper clips |
| door magnets | waterproof glue |
| dowels | strong magnets |
| balsa wood | wooden skewer |
| metal thumbtacks | glass baking dish |

## To make the cork boats

**1** Make the sails out of poster board. You can make one triangular sail by cutting out two triangles and sticking them back to back with a wire mast in the middle.

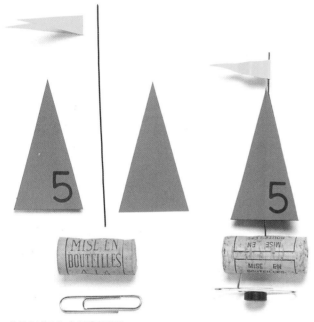

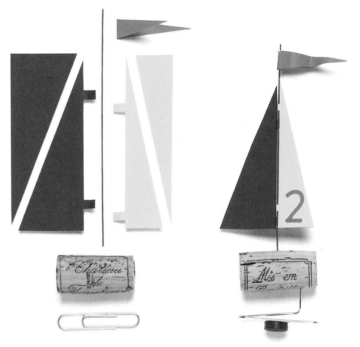

### MAKE it WORK!

There are two different kinds of magnetic boats to make. The cork boats work by magnet-to-magnet attraction. The boat magnets are close to the bottom of the water container, so the boats can be pulled around by a small bar magnet attached to the end of a stick. The balsa-wood boat has thumbtacks pushed into its keel and needs a stronger magnet with a force field that will attract through shallow water.

*Even though the ancient Greeks knew of magnets, for hundreds of years people did not know how to make magnets for themselves. Not until the nineteenth century were magnetism and its close connection to electricity properly understood.*

**2** To make a more complex rig, cut a rectangle of poster board diagonally, leaving enough poster board on the long outside edge to make two tabs. Attach the sail to a piece of wire with these tabs.

**3** Push the wire mast into a cork. **Be very careful!** Don't stab yourself with the wire. Top the mast with a flag made from a folded strip of paper of a contrasting color.

**4** Unbend a paper clip as shown above. Push one end into the underside of the cork and glue a small door magnet onto the other end, using waterproof glue.

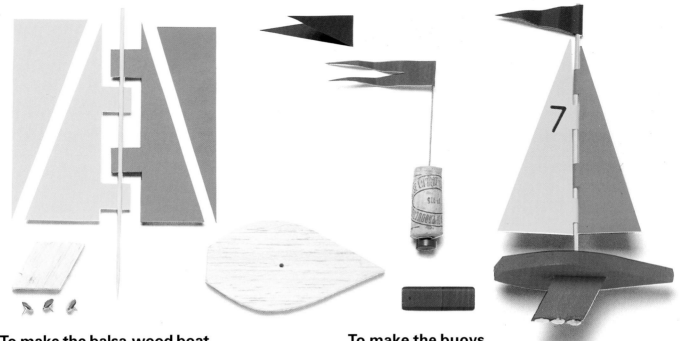

## To make the balsa-wood boat

**1** Ask an adult to help you cut a deck and keel out of balsa wood as shown above.

**2** Stick a wooden skewer into the center of the deck to make a mast.

**3** Make sails and flags as for the cork boats, but in a larger size.

**4** Glue the boat together with waterproof glue and paint it. Push three thumbtacks into the bottom of the keel.

## To make the buoys

Put a short piece of wire into a cork and top it with a colored flag. Stick a door magnet to the bottom of the cork with waterproof glue.

*The ancient Greeks told a story about an imaginary island of magnetic mountains that could pull the iron nails out of passing ships!*

Earth is actually a giant magnet, and its strongest points are near the North Pole and the South Pole. No one really knows why Earth is a magnet, but its force field extends thousands of miles into space. Any magnet on Earth allowed to swing freely will always point to the north—which is very handy if you need to find out where you are!

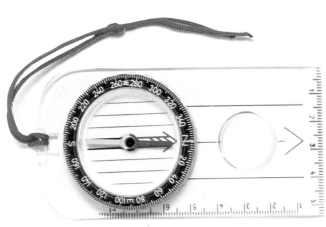

## MAKE it WORK!

Every magnet has two points called **poles** where its magnetic force is strongest. Because magnets always line up with magnet Earth, the end of a magnet that points south is called the south pole. This is the basic principle that makes a compass work. Although some fancy compasses can give very precise readings, even a simple compass will let you know if you are heading in the right direction. All you need is a magnetized needle that can swing freely.

### To make a water compass you will need

| | |
|---|---|
| old yogurt container | magnet |
| needle | slice of cork |
| cardboard | protractor |
| tape | scissors |

**1** Cut out a circle of cardboard and cut a hole in the center just smaller than the opening of the yogurt container.

**2** Using a protractor, divide the circle into accurate quarters and label the four compass points: North, South, East, and West.

**3** Make the needle magnetic by stroking it with one end of a magnet about twenty times. Always stroke in the same direction. Tape the needle onto a thin slice of cork.

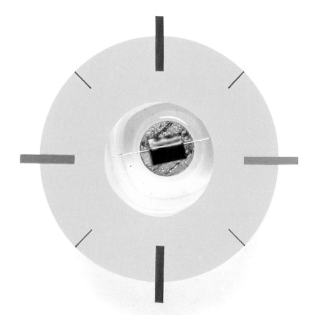

**4** Fill the yogurt container with water and float the cork in it. When the needle has settled to the north, tape the cardboard ring to the container so that the needle points to the *North* label. Check your readings against a real compass.

*The poles of magnets react to one another just like the two kinds of electric charge. Opposite poles attract—and like poles repel.*

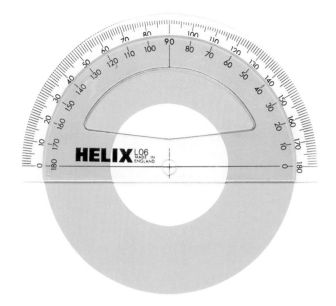

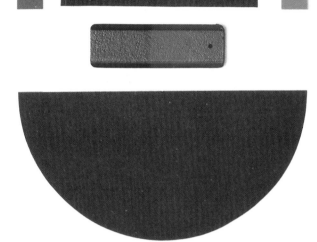

## For two simple compasses you will need

| | |
|---|---|
| cardboard | wooden skewer |
| magnet | needles and thread |
| jar | tape |

Fold a strip of cardboard and tape a magnetized needle to it.

## Jar compass

Suspend the compass strip in a glass jar, using a straw or a pencil and some thread. This compass will also work outdoors because the jar protects the needle from the wind.

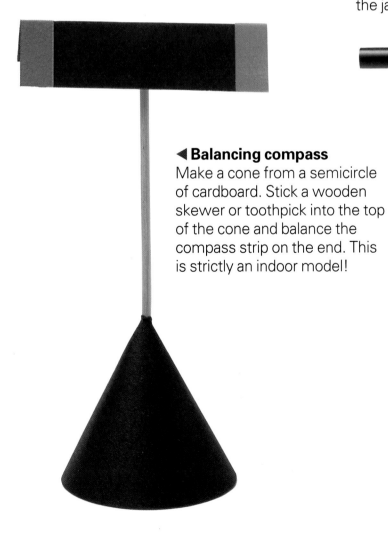

### ◀ Balancing compass

Make a cone from a semicircle of cardboard. Stick a wooden skewer or toothpick into the top of the cone and balance the compass strip on the end. This is strictly an indoor model!

You can actually see a magnetic field by laying a piece of paper over a magnet and sprinkling iron filings onto it. The magnet's force field is strong enough to work through the paper, and the filings will act like tiny magnets, clustering around the north and south poles where the force is strongest.

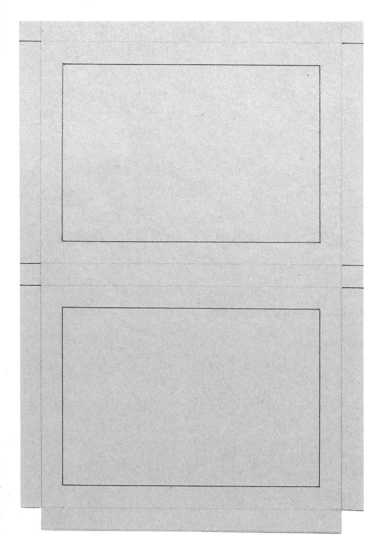

▲ Here you can see the force field at work. The iron filings form a pattern of lines running from pole to pole. These lines are called lines of induction, and they show us the invisible force field of the magnet.

## MAKE it WORK!
Use the power of magnetism to draw pictures with iron filings.

### You will need
| | |
|---|---|
| cardboard | clear acetate sheets |
| rubber bands | iron filings and a magnet |
| scissors | clear tape |

**Be careful!** Iron filings are dangerous. Don't breathe them in or swallow any, and don't lick your fingers after touching them.

**1** Cut out a rectangle of cardboard and mark it as shown. Cut along the red lines and fold and glue along the pencil lines to make a box.

**2** Take two pieces of clear acetate and cut them slightly bigger than the windows of the drawing box. Tape them in place with clear tape.

**3** Draw some silly faces on sheets of white paper, leaving out the hair.

**4** Put a face card inside the box and shake iron filings on top of it. Snap the box shut with the rubber bands. Put the drawing box on a flat surface. Now you can "draw" the hair on your face by passing a magnet over the acetate.

*A new kind of train in Europe runs on the principle of magnetic levitation. Both the track and parts of the train are magnetic. The train works on the pull and push of magnets that repel and attract. The train floats above the track because the train and the track repel one another. There are no wheels to wear out or to cause **friction** and slow the train down.*

Electricity and magnetism are closely related to each other. Both are caused by the movement of electrons, and every electric current has its own magnetic field. This magnetic force in electricity can be used to make powerful **electromagnets** that can be turned on and off at the flick of a switch.

## MAKE it WORK!

This crane uses an electromagnetic coil. The magnetic field produced by a single wire isn't very strong, but when electricity flows through a wire coiled around a conductor, the coil becomes a powerful magnet.

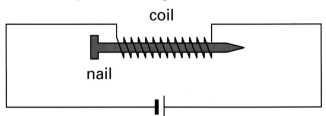

coil

nail

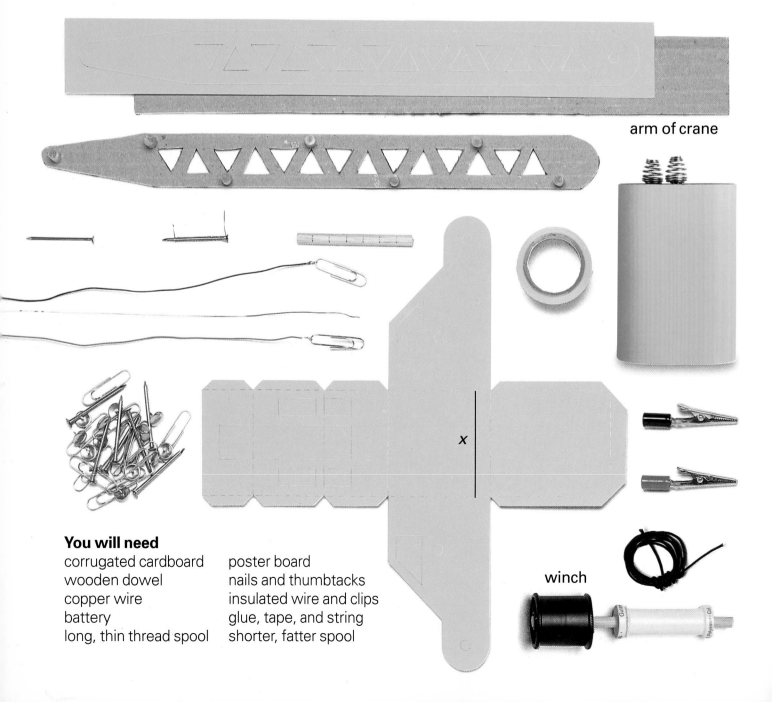

arm of crane

*x*

winch

### You will need

| | |
|---|---|
| corrugated cardboard | poster board |
| wooden dowel | nails and thumbtacks |
| copper wire | insulated wire and clips |
| battery | glue, tape, and string |
| long, thin thread spool | shorter, fatter spool |

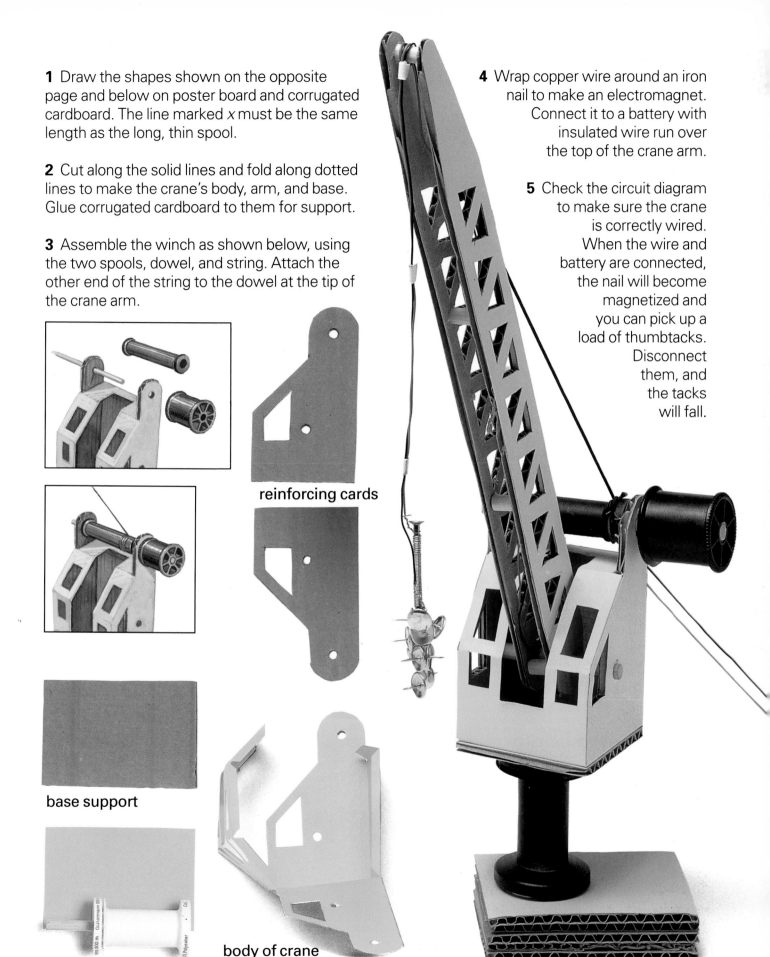

**1** Draw the shapes shown on the opposite page and below on poster board and corrugated cardboard. The line marked *x* must be the same length as the long, thin spool.

**2** Cut along the solid lines and fold along dotted lines to make the crane's body, arm, and base. Glue corrugated cardboard to them for support.

**3** Assemble the winch as shown below, using the two spools, dowel, and string. Attach the other end of the string to the dowel at the tip of the crane arm.

**4** Wrap copper wire around an iron nail to make an electromagnet. Connect it to a battery with insulated wire run over the top of the crane arm.

**5** Check the circuit diagram to make sure the crane is correctly wired. When the wire and battery are connected, the nail will become magnetized and you can pick up a load of thumbtacks. Disconnect them, and the tacks will fall.

reinforcing cards

base support

body of crane

Electrical energy can be converted into mechanical energy, that is, energy that can pull and push and make things go. When electricity flows through the wires inside this motor, it makes them magnetic. The coil of wires becomes an electromagnet. It is attracted to fixed magnets inside the motor, which makes it spin around and around.

**MAKE it WORK!**
In this electric motor, a copper coil (the electromagnet) is connected to a battery by a clever little device called a **commutator**. The commutator brushes up against the wire ends of the electromagnetic coil, so that the electric current passes through, but the connections are loose enough to allow the coil to rotate freely.

As the coil turns, the connections of the commutator switch from side to side, so the direction of the electric current keeps changing. As the direction of the current changes, the poles of the electromagnet change sides, too. The electromagnet is always attracted to the farthest fixed magnet and so it keeps on spinning and spinning.

coil (electromagnet)

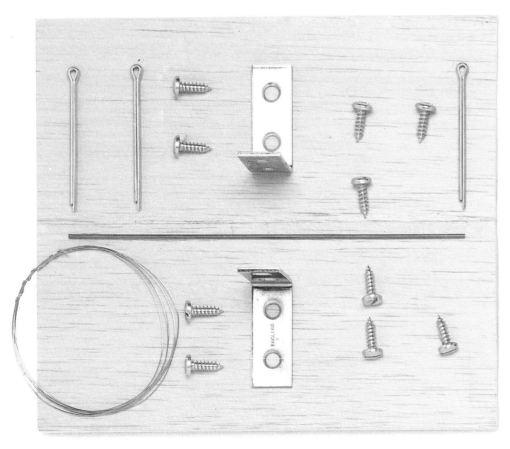

**You will need**

| | | | |
|---|---|---|---|
| wood for the base | utility knife | copper wire | 2 strong magnets |
| 2 angle brackets | screws | balsa-wood block | electrical tape |
| thin copper tube | split-pin clips | alligator clips/paper clips | clear tape |
| | metal spindle | battery | |

**1** Cut the base board out of a piece of balsa wood, or find a piece of soft wood. You could paint it a bright color.

**2** Ask an adult to drill a hole through the length of a small block of balsa wood. The hole should be wide enough for the copper tube to fit through.

**4** Screw the angle brackets to the base board. Stick on the magnets, positioning them so that they attract one another. Ask an adult to drill three holes along the center of the board to stand the split pins in.

**5** Thread the metal spindle through the split pins and the balsa-wood block so that the coil is suspended and can turn easily.

**6** Now make the commutator. The wires from the battery need to touch the ends of wire from the electromagnetic coil without stopping the coil from spinning. Strip some of the plastic from the ends of the wires and bend them inward. Follow the illustration on the left.

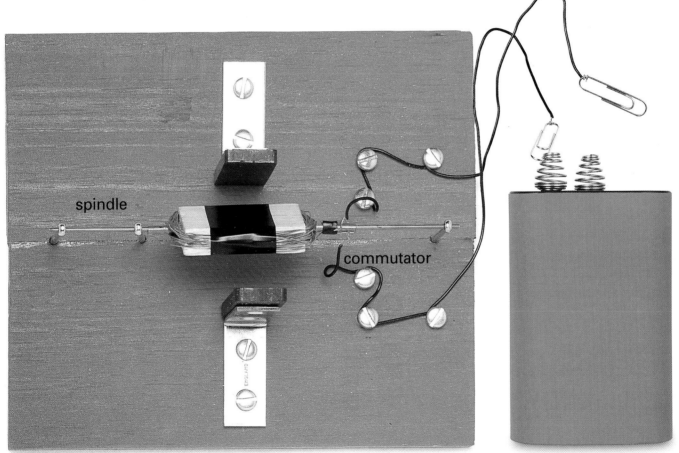

spindle

commutator

**3** Ask an adult to cut grooves along two edges of the balsa-wood block with a utility knife. Wrap copper wire tightly around the block. Insulate one end of the copper tube with clear tape. Fix the ends of the copper wire in place over the clear tape with insulating tape.

**7** Screw the electrical wires into position so that the commutator connection is firmly fixed in place and cannot move. You may have to experiment a bit to get the screws positioned in the right place. Now connect the battery!

Our simple electric motor turned a spindle around and around. One of the most direct and efficient ways to use this energy is to attach a propeller to the spindle. Boats are often driven by propellers in this way.

**1** Make a balsa-wood frame for the hull and deck as shown on the right. Ask an adult to drill holes for the dowels. Glue them in place with waterproof glue. Screw the electric motor in position. Paint the hull and deck with waterproof paint.

**2** Connect wires to the motor.

### MAKE it WORK!
This propeller-driven boat makes good use of energy. It is designed with a propeller that drives through air rather than water because air is thinner than water and easier to move.

### You will need
6-volt battery
screws
balsa wood
thin dowels
electric motor
modeling clay
stiff metal wire
waterproof glue
model propeller
waterproof paint
long wires and clips
poster board and tape

### To make the buoys
Push a couple of large nails into a cork. Add a flag and leave your buoy to float on the water.

**3** Make the framework for the rudder by asking and adult to bend the metal wire as shown at right. Drill shallow holes in the wood for the metal wire to sit in. Now cut a rectangle of poster board for the rudder and tape it into place on the metal wire as shown.

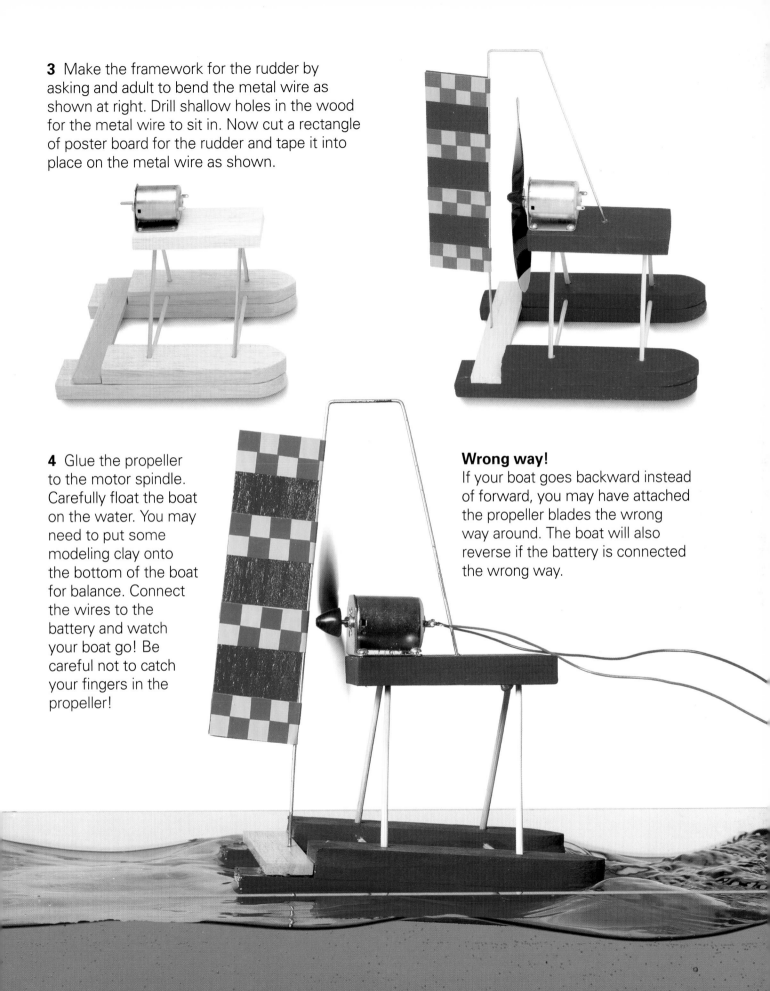

**4** Glue the propeller to the motor spindle. Carefully float the boat on the water. You may need to put some modeling clay onto the bottom of the boat for balance. Connect the wires to the battery and watch your boat go! Be careful not to catch your fingers in the propeller!

**Wrong way!**
If your boat goes backward instead of forward, you may have attached the propeller blades the wrong way around. The boat will also reverse if the battery is connected the wrong way.

Modern high-speed electric trains are run by large electric motors. Power is supplied by overhead wires or electrified tracks. Electric trains use energy more efficiently because they don't have to haul heavy loads of fuel.

### You will need

| | |
|---|---|
| battery | beads |
| wooden dowels | paper clips |
| electric motor | slices of cork |
| poster board | upholstery pins |
| copper wire | 3 thin copper strips |
| balsa wood | corrugated cardboard |
| 7 plastic bottle tops | door magnets |
| screws, thin nails, and glue | |

**1** Ask an adult to help you cut out the balsa-wood base of the engine. Then glue and nail the two roof supports into position as shown. Stick the upholstery pins into the supports.

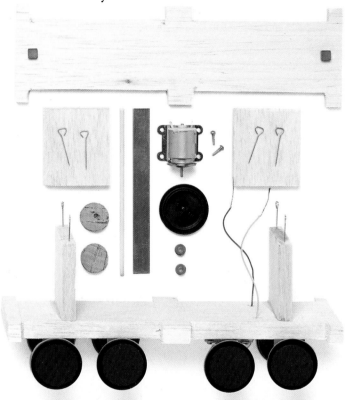

### MAKE it WORK!
This model electric train works just like the real thing. The motor is on board, but the power is supplied through power lines overhead and is passed down to the motor through the upholstery pins.

**2** Glue a plastic bottle top to the spindle of the electric motor, making a wheel. Screw the motor to the base of the train, and then pass two wires from the motor up through the base and clip them to the upholstery pins.

**3** Ask an adult to drill four holes into each copper strip and bend them as shown to make the axle holders. Drill holes through the base and screw the axle holders into place.

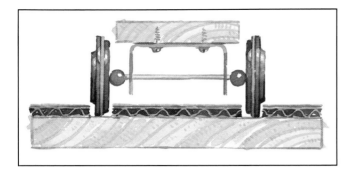

**4** Make the axles by feeding the dowels through the axle holders. Then glue the beads and bottle tops to the ends of the axles to make the wheels.

**6** Lay down three long strips of corrugated cardboard to make two grooves for your train to run along. Add balsa-wood arches overhead and string a length of wire between them, threading it through the upholstery pins. Connect the overhead wires to the battery and watch your train go!

### Extra cars
Try making different kinds of cars for your train. They don't need motors or wires, but you can make wheels and bases as you did for the engine. Join them with small door magnets behind cork buffers.

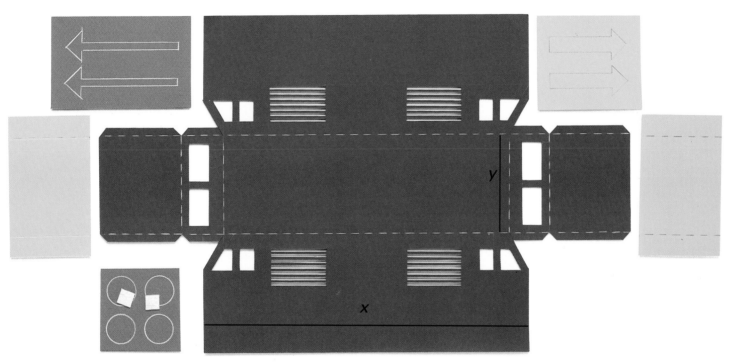

**5** Draw a pattern on the poster board as shown, making sure that line *x* is as long as the balsa-wood base and line *y* is the same width as the base. Assemble the body of the train and fit it over the base.

### Running backward and forward
To make your train run the opposite way, just reverse the connections on the battery.

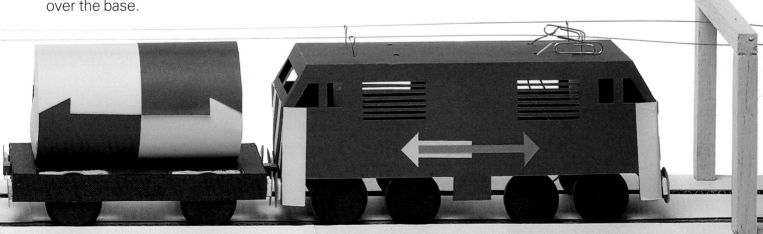

Electric motors range from the very small to the enormous. There are small battery-operated motors in model trains and clocks, but some electric motors in factories need a power supply so strong that it has to come directly from the power station.

## MAKE it WORK!

See for yourself what happens if you change the supply to an electric motor. Build a spin-o-matico to make colorful patterns with paint. Compare the different results you get with different batteries.

**1** Glue the two containers together, bottom to bottom, so you have two open ends. The top one will hold the paint, and the bottom one will hold the motor and wires.

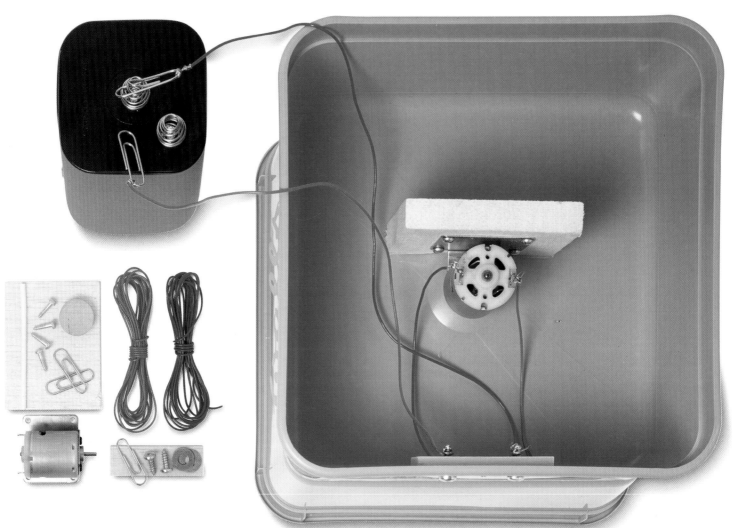

### You will need

2 plastic containers
2 different-sized batteries
screws and washers
slice of cork
poster paint
glue and rubber cement

electric motor
paper clips
wire
wood
glossy cardboard
alligator clips

**2** Poke the spindle of the electric motor through the center of the bottom container (the motor one), so it sticks up through the bottom of the top one (the paint holder). Screw the electric motor to a small piece of wood to hold it in place, and glue the wood to the container.

**3** Make an on/off switch like the one shown on page 66, using a paper clip and two screws. Screw the paper clip to the outside of the container and onto a small piece of wood inside the container for support.

**4** Wire the more powerful battery up to the motor, including the on/off switch in the circuit. To connect the wires to the switch, twist the ends of the wires around the screws, or attach them with alligator clips.

**5** Turn the containers over. Put a slice of cork over the top of the electric spindle that is poking up through the container. Test the motor to see if the cork spins when you switch it on.

**6** Take a piece of cardboard and stick it onto the cork using a dab of rubber cement.

**7** Switch the motor on and dribble paint onto the whirling card to make a pattern. You can also use a paint brush if you want to.

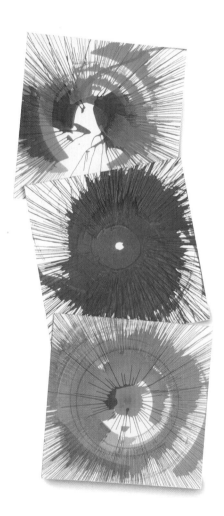

▲ Try doing some paintings using less power. Replace the powerful battery with the weaker one. How does the reduced power affect your finished painting?

*When something is spinning very fast, the outside spins much faster than the inside. The force that seems to push everything toward the outside is called centrifugal force.*

# Sound

Did you know that sounds can blow out candles and crack glass? Or that bats use sounds to "see" and find their way around? Have you ever wondered how different musical instruments produce completely different sounds?

## MAKE it WORK!
Start experimenting with sound. Find out how sound waves are made, how they travel, and some of the surprising things they do.

## You will need
Most of the activities in this book use simple equipment, such as cardboard, glue and odds and ends. However, you will find some specialist equipment useful.

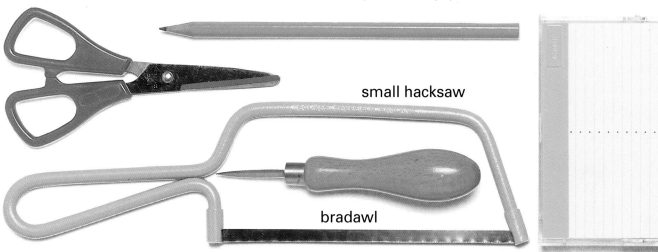

small hacksaw

bradawl

Investigating sound is part of the science of **physics**. Sound is a kind of energy that flows through the air in invisible waves. Everything that makes the air move, from the rustling of a leaf to the pounding of a big bass drum, sets off **sound waves**, and creates a different kind of sound.

**Small hacksaw and bradawl** Some of the activities include making simple wooden supports or structures. You should always ask an adult to help if you are using saws, utility knives or other sharp tools.

**Cardboard tubes** These are handy for making musical instruments. You can use the insides of aluminum foil rolls or cardboard tubes made for carrying posters.

**Music manuscript paper** This is useful for writing down musical notes.

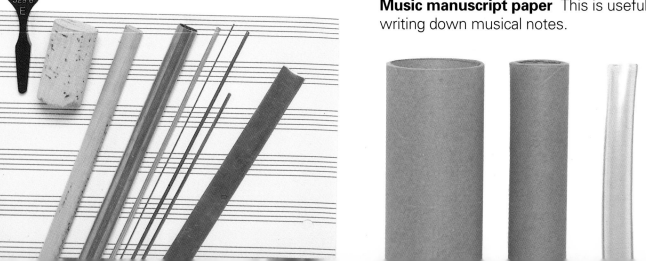

**Copper wire** This will be needed for making a simple radio and a telephone. Sound waves can be turned into an electrical pulse and then transferred along the wire. You can buy copper wire at any hobby shop or electrical supplier.

**Balloons and rubber bands** Some of the projects involve making a drum. Rubber from a balloon makes an excellent drumhead, and elastic bands will hold the rubber in place without tearing it.

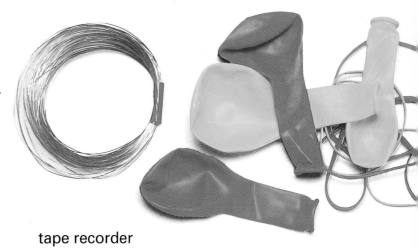

tape recorder

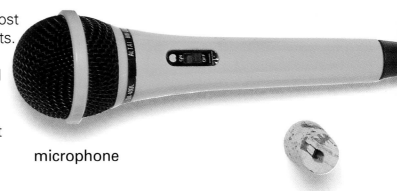

earphones

**Tape recorder** A simple tape recorder is the most useful piece of equipment for sound experiments. Ideally, you will need a small tape recorder or personal stereo, along with a microphone, small headphones and some blank cassettes.

**Plastic tubing and corks** These can be bought from hobby shops.

microphone

*When we hear a noise, the sound waves usually travel to our ears through air, but sound can move through other substances too. Whales, for instance, hear a wide range of sound waves that move through water.*

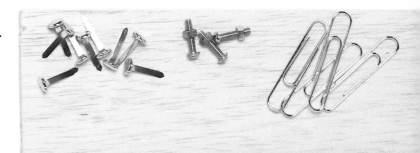

We hear sound when a moving object makes the air **vibrate**. These vibrations travel through the air in the form of waves, and are picked up by our ears as sounds. The shape of the sound wave depends on the **pitch** of the sound. Low-pitched sounds are deep and rumbling, like a big bass drum. High-pitched sounds are shrill and piercing, like a whistle.

## MAKE it WORK!

If you could see air, it would look like a huge floating soup of gas particles. Low noises would make ripples that are far apart, and high-pitched sounds would make waves that are very close together. In fact, sound waves in air are invisible, but you can certainly prove they exist. Here are two ways to observe their effects.

### For the sugar drum you will need

| | |
|---|---|
| a cake tin | sugar |
| a wooden spoon | a balloon |
| large rubber bands | a baking pan |

**1** Cut out a circle of balloon rubber. Stretch it over the cake tin and secure it with rubber bands.

**2** Sprinkle a little sugar on the top of the drum.

**3** Hold the baking pan above the drum and hit it with the wooden spoon. As the sound waves reach your ear, you hear the sound of the spoon on the pan. When those same waves hit the drumhead, they make it vibrate and you can see the sugar dancing up and down.

◀ Try holding the baking pan closer to the drum and then farther away from it. Does this affect how much the sugar moves?

## For the sound cannon you will need

| | |
|---|---|
| a cardboard tube | candles |
| a piece of plywood | long nails |
| a plastic bag or a balloon | rubber bands |

**1** Ask an adult to help you hammer three nails through a piece of wood. Turn the wood over and push a candle onto each nail.

**2** Take a piece of cardboard tube. The inside of a roll of aluminum foil will work well too.

**3** Stretch a circle of balloon rubber or plastic bag over each end of the tube and secure each with rubber bands.

**4** Make a little hole in the plastic stretched over one end of the tube.

**5** Light the candles.

**6** Point the end of the sound cannon with the hole in it at one of the candles. Hold it just a few inches away.

**7** Tap the other end with your finger. The vibrations you make by tapping the drumhead travel to your ear as sound waves. The same vibrations move down the tube and push the air through the little hole at the opposite end, blowing out the candles.

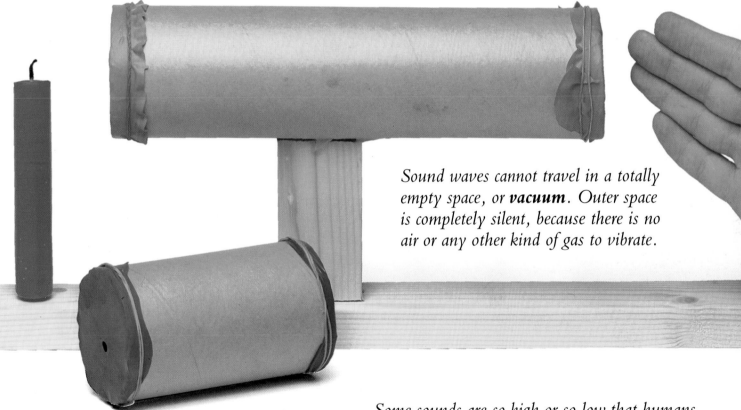

*Sound waves cannot travel in a totally empty space, or **vacuum**. Outer space is completely silent, because there is no air or any other kind of gas to vibrate.*

*Scientists measure sound waves by the number of times they make the air vibrate each second. One vibration, or cycle, per second is called one **Hertz** (Hz). When you hear a 700 Hz noise, the sound waves are hitting your eardrum 700 times per second. Scientists also measure other types of waves, such as light waves or radio waves, in Hertz.*

*Some sounds are so high or so low that humans cannot hear them. We are unable to make out sounds that have a frequency above roughly 20,000 Hz, or below 20 Hz. However, many animals have a much wider hearing range than humans. Bats and dogs, for instance, both pick up much higher sounds than we do. There are even special dog whistles that give out a high-pitched noise which only dogs can hear.*

Our ears are specially designed to pick up vibrations in the air and change them into **nerve pulses** which our brains then understand as sounds. The working parts of our ears are actually inside our skulls. The flaps that stick out on either side of our heads are just funnels used to collect sounds and pass them along to the **eardrum**.

## MAKE it WORK!

Make your own working model of a human ear. The eardrum vibrates, moving three small bones inside the inner ear. These bones in turn move a fluid through a curly pipe called the **cochlea**. The cochlea is lined with minute hairs, and as the fluid moves, so do the hairs, sending tiny sound impulses along the nerves to the brain.

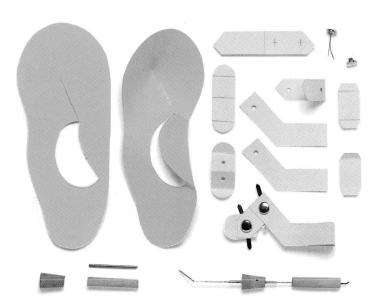

## You will need

| | |
|---|---|
| wood and nails | two cork stoppers |
| thin dowels | one piece of longer, |
| rough twine | thinner cork |
| plastic tubing | thin poster board |
| paper fasteners | stiff wire, a balloon |
| a cardboard tube | tape and rubber cement |
| thin copper tubing | food coloring |

**1** Take a piece of cardboard tube and cut out part of one side as shown. Place a circle of balloon rubber over one end, fixing it securely with rubber bands. This will be the eardrum.

**2** Make the bones that are connected to the eardrum – the **malleus**, the **incus** and the **stapes**. In the model, these bones are made from pieces of poster board. Cut out and fold the shapes shown in the photograph. Then glue and fix them together with paper fasteners as shown in the diagram on the right.

**3** Stick the flaps of the cardboard malleus onto the rubber of the eardrum with rubber cement.

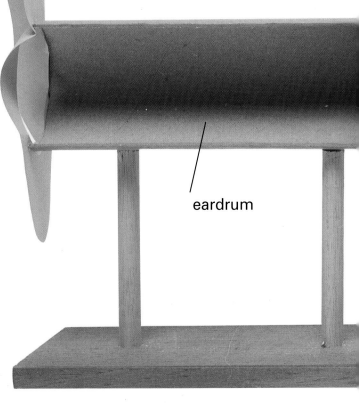

eardrum

**4** Cut a piece of flexible, transparent plastic tubing and thread a slightly shorter piece of string through it. Use a rough kind of twine, made out of natural fibers. The plastic tube is the cochlea, and the fibers on the twine are the tiny hairs that send nerve pulses to the brain.

Making the inner ear

Then thread the stiff wire through the copper tubing and stick it into the thinner piece of cork as shown.

**6** Push the cork and wire mechanism into one end of the plastic tube. Almost fill the tube with water, add several drops of food coloring, and use the remaining cork to stop up the other end.

**5** Connect the "bones" to the "cochlea." Ask an adult to drill a narrow hole in one cork stopper and push a small piece of thin copper tubing through the hole.

**7** Make a wooden base and put the separate parts of the model together, holding them up on dowel supports. Glue the wire to the cardboard "stapes" and twist and tape the "cochlea" into a spiral shape.

**8** Make an outer ear shape from colored poster board, and glue it to the free end of the tube.

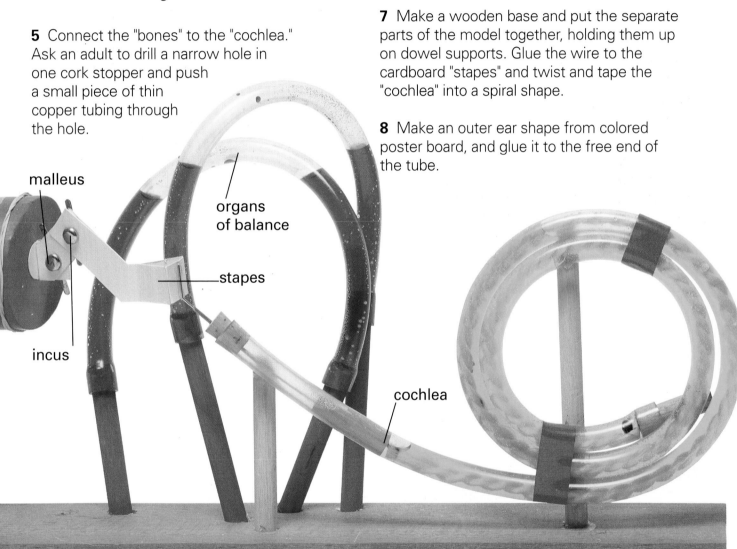

malleus

organs of balance

stapes

incus

cochlea

▲ Ears are important for things other than hearing. They also help us to keep our balance. You can make your model ear even more authentic by adding semicircular tubes filled with colored water. These represent the fluid canals that are our organs of balance.

**Operating the model**
To watch your model work, tap lightly on the inside of the eardrum to make it vibrate as though it had been hit by a sound wave. Can you see what happens to the little hairs on the string inside the cochlea tube?

Have you ever wondered why you have two ears, placed on either side of your head? It's to help you tell which direction a sound is coming from. Unless a sound comes from directly in front of you, one ear will always pick up more of it than the other. Your brain uses the different information coming from each ear to work out the direction of the sound.

**MAKE it WORK!**
To find out where a sound is coming from, we usually turn our heads until both ears hear the sound equally and the sound is "in focus." Make this game and test whether your ears have a good sense of direction.

**You will need**
large sheets of
    colored paper or thin poster board
a pencil, scissors and string
some friends
a blindfold

**1** Take a large sheet of paper and fold it in half. Attach a pencil to one end of a piece of string and fasten the other end of the string to the piece of paper at a corner along the fold.

**2** Use the string and pencil like a compass to draw an arc. Then cut along the line, and unfold the paper to give you a semicircle. Repeat with another piece of paper the same size.

**3** Put the two semicircles together to make a whole circle. If you wish, you can divide the semicircles into segments and make alternate colors. Then cut out a paper arrow.

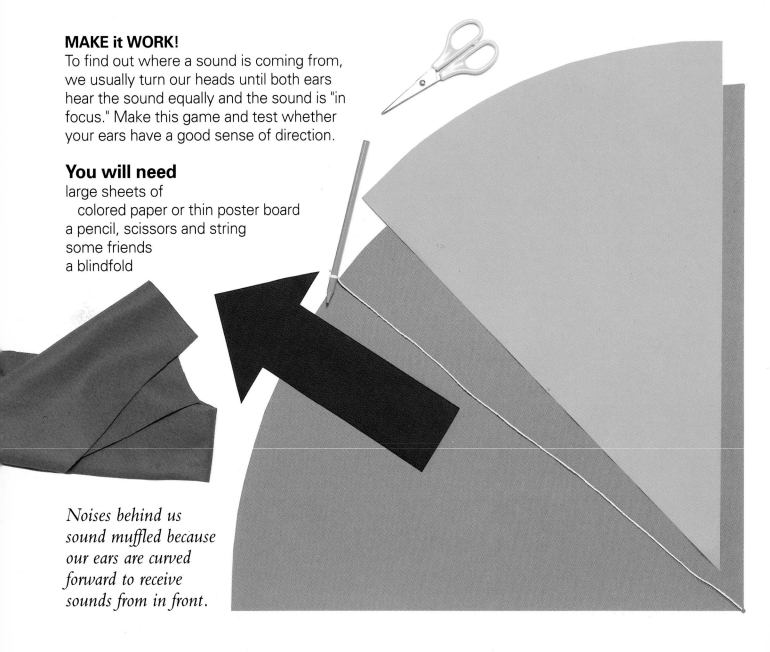

*Noises behind us sound muffled because our ears are curved forward to receive sounds from in front.*

*Compared with light, sound waves travel quite slowly – light moves almost a million times faster than sound. That's why, during a thunder storm, we see a flash of lightning before we hear a clap of thunder, even though they are both, in fact, caused at exactly the same time.*

## ▼ Playing the game

This is a game for three to five people. One person volunteers to wear a blindfold and sits in the middle of the circle. The other players stand or sit silently around the circle, and someone makes a gentle noise, such as clicking his or her fingers. The blindfolded person points the arrow in the direction they think the sound is coming from. Each player can have a turn at being blindfolded. Whose ears have the best sense of direction?

Instead of poster board, you could make the circle out of felt or another material.

▶ Ask a friend to stand at the other side of a field or playground, holding up a handkerchief. (The farther away your friend, the better the experiment will work – a pair of binoculars could help here.) Tell the friend to shout and drop the handkerchief at exactly the same time. You should see the handkerchief begin to fall before you hear the shout.

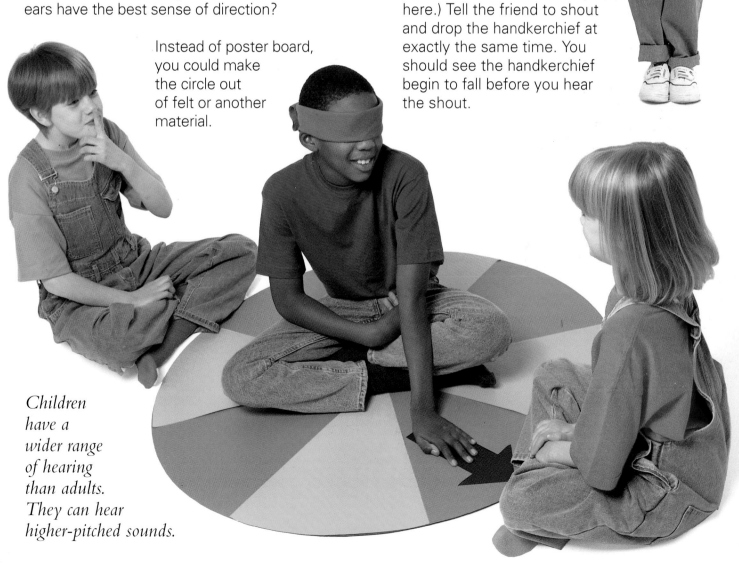

*Children have a wider range of hearing than adults. They can hear higher-pitched sounds.*

Our ears pick up the sound waves traveling through air, but, in fact, sound waves can travel through all kinds of substances. Whales, for instance, hear sound waves in water. And sound can even pass through a solid object, such as wood, if it is made to vibrate. However, sound doesn't pass very well from one type of substance to another. If you shout at a brick wall, not much of the sound gets from the air through the wall and out the other side. Instead, the sound waves bounce back off the wall again.

## Angles of bounce

Sound waves in air will bounce off a flat, solid object at the same angle as they hit it – just like a bouncing ball off a wall. If, however, the sound waves are bounced off a surface that is soft or bumpy, the waves will break up and fade away.

## You will need

thick poster board    modeling clay
a utility knife and ruler    an egg carton
cardboard tubes
a tape recorder and microphone
a clock or watch with a very soft tick

## MAKE it WORK!

In this experiment, you can control the path of the sound waves by directing them along cardboard tubes. The tubes hold the sound together, making it louder because the sound waves can't spread out and get lost in the air around them.

**1** Take four equal pieces of cardboard tube, and cut three squares out of a piece of thick, smooth poster board.

**2** Use modeling clay to secure the cardboard tubes and the squares of poster board in position as shown below. Each tube must be placed at exactly the same angle to the squares as the others have been.

**3** Measure the distance in a straight line between one end of the zig-zag and the other.

**4** Set up your clock or watch away from the tubes, and record it ticking across the distance you have measured. Your microphone will pick up only a faint sound, or no sound at all.

**5** Now position the clock at one end of the zig-zag, and record the sound that comes out of the other end.

**6** If all of your tubes are positioned at the same angle, you should be able to record the ticking sound clearly. The sound waves travel down one tube, bounce on and off the reflector card at the end, and continue back down the next tube.

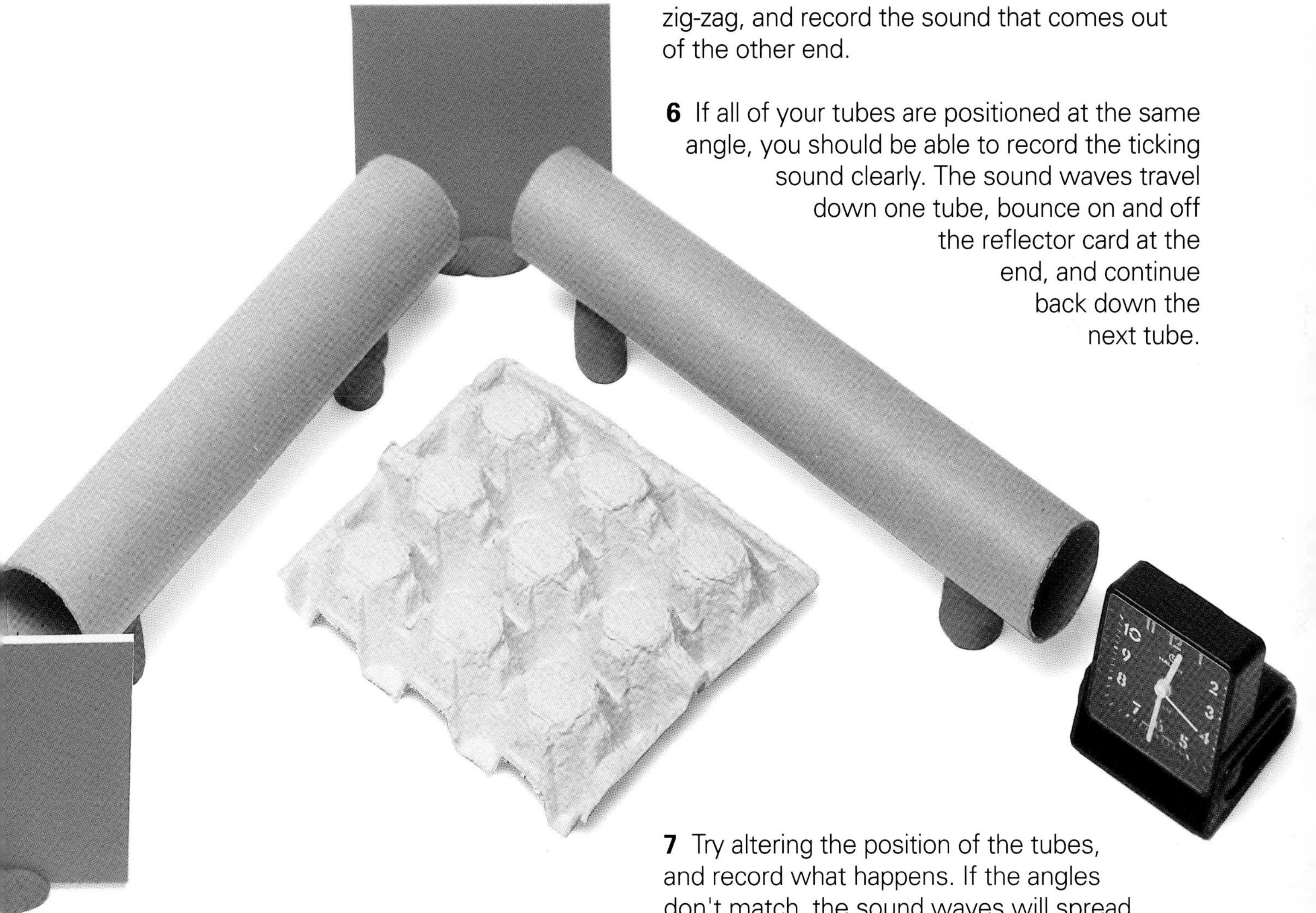

**7** Try altering the position of the tubes, and record what happens. If the angles don't match, the sound waves will spread out into the surrounding air, getting weaker and weaker.

### Deadening sound

Put the cardboard tubes back in their original zig-zag positions and then experiment with reflector cards made out of different materials. Cut some squares out of an old egg carton, so you can test the effect that a bumpy, uneven surface has on sound waves.

*Architects use their knowledge of bouncing sound waves when they design new buildings. A noisy restaurant can be made much quieter by covering the floor, walls and ceiling with soft fabrics and bumpy surfaces to deaden the sound. But the stage and walls of a concert hall can be built to reflect sound waves, so that the music travels clearly toward where the audience is sitting.*

Before electronic hearing aids were invented, people who had difficulty hearing used an ear trumpet. They would put the narrow end of the ear trumpet to their ear, and if someone spoke clearly into the wide end, they could hear that person's voice more clearly. The ear trumpet **amplified** the sounds, or made them louder.

The simplest amplifier is a big cone. It can be used to send out sounds or to listen to them. When it is used to send sounds, the cone holds the sound waves together, so they don't spread out in the air so quickly. When a cone is used to listen, like the old-fashioned ear trumpet, it collects sound waves from the air and directs them into the ear so they sound louder.

## You will need

thin colored poster board    glue or tape
flexible plastic tubing    scissors
two plastic funnels

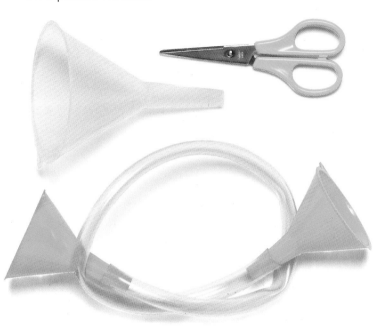

## MAKE it WORK!

You can make some instruments to amplify sound waves. Doctors use a special listening device called a **stethoscope** to hear inside their patients' bodies. Normally, we can't hear the quiet gurgles and thumps made by our bodies, but the stethoscope picks up the sound waves and leads them directly into the doctor's ear.

### Making a stethoscope

Take a piece of plastic tubing that fits neatly over the narrow ends of the two funnels. Attach a funnel to each end.

Ask a friend to hold one funnel over his or her chest, put the other funnel to your ear and listen carefully. You will be able to hear your friend's heartbeat.

*The loudness of a sound is measured by the force with which the sound wave pushes the air. The units of measurement are called **decibels** – named after the scientist and inventor Alexander Graham Bell.*

## Making an ear trumpet and a megaphone

**1** Take a sheet of thin, colored poster board and roll it into a cone shape. One end should be wide, to collect sound waves, and the other end should be narrow enough to fit into your ear.

**2** Make the megaphone the same way, but the narrow end should be slightly larger so that you can speak into it.

**3** Once you have the right cone shapes, tape or glue the poster board. Trim the ends and decorate the cones with colored paper shapes of bright, contrasting colors.

**4** To test the megaphone, ask a friend to stand far enough away so you can't hear each other's voices. Then speak normally through the cone.

**5** To test the ear trumpet, point it toward a quiet noise. You will be able to hear the sound more clearly. **Be careful!** Never shout at anyone down an ear trumpet. You could damage their eardrum.

*On the decibel scale, 0 is absolute silence. A falling leaf would measure 20 decibels, a conversation about 50 and a clap of thunder 110. Above 140 decibels, sounds become painful and may damage the eardrum.*

Sound waves can be converted from sound energy into electrical energy and back again. That's how sounds can be carried over long distances by the telephone. The sound waves are turned into electrical pulses, which travel through the telephone wire to the receiver – just like the nerve pulses that carry sounds from our ears to our brains.

**MAKE it WORK!**
Modern telephones use carbon granules to convert sound waves into electrical pulses. However, you can make a simple telephone for yourself, using magnets and copper wire.

When you speak into the paper cup, the paper drumhead vibrates and causes the magnet to bounce up and down inside a coil of copper wire. This movement causes an electrical charge, which passes down the wire. At the other end of the wire, another copper coil, magnet and drumhead convert the electrical pulses back into sound waves.

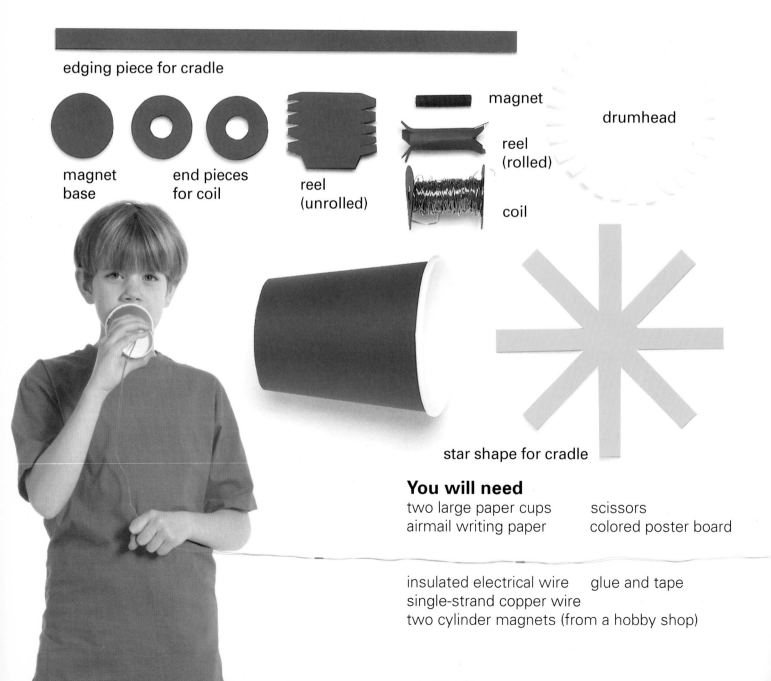

edging piece for cradle

magnet base

end pieces for coil

reel (unrolled)

magnet

reel (rolled)

coil

drumhead

star shape for cradle

**You will need**

| | |
|---|---|
| two large paper cups | scissors |
| airmail writing paper | colored poster board |

insulated electrical wire    glue and tape
single-strand copper wire
two cylinder magnets (from a hobby shop)

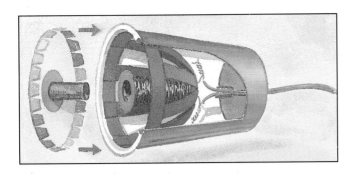

**1** First make a copper coil. Cut and glue the pieces of poster board as shown to make a reel that will fit neatly around a cylinder magnet. Wind a long piece of copper wire around the reel forty or fifty times.

▲ cylinder magnet attached to drumhead

▲ cradle

**2** Cut a star shape and edging piece out of thick poster board as shown. Fold the spokes of the star shape and glue the edging piece around them to make a cradle.

**3** Pass two equal pieces of insulated wire through the bottom of a paper cup and connect them to the end of the copper coil. Leave the

connecting wire long enough to stretch at least across a large room.

**4** Now assemble a paper cup receiver. First, glue the coil into the cradle. Glue the cradle inside the paper cup as shown.

**5** Cut a drumhead out of thin airmail paper. Glue the magnet to a small, circular magnet base cut from poster board and glue that onto the back of the paper drumhead. Then glue the drumhead in place. Check that the magnet fits neatly inside the reel, but has room to move freely up and down.

**6** Repeat steps 1–5 to make the second receiver. For step 3, use the other end of the wire that you connected to the first copper coil.

**7** To talk into the telephone, cup your hands around the cup and talk right at the drumhead. To listen, hold the drumhead up to your ear.

Sound was first recorded by a machine called a **phonograph** – a kind of early record player. A needle was attached to a drumhead, stretched across the narrow end of a sound horn. When someone shouted into the horn, the needle would vibrate. As the needle bounced up and down, it recorded the sound waves as grooves on a cylinder coated in wax or tinfoil.

### Tape recordings

Sound recording techniques have come a long way since the days of the phonograph. Sound is now recorded onto magnetic tape. In the tape recorder, the sound waves are turned into electric impulses. These are stored on the tape as a sequence of different magnetic blips.

### MAKE it WORK!

A microphone is a kind of electric ear. It turns sound waves into electric signals. However, it may have trouble picking up sounds not made close by. You can improve a simple microphone by putting it inside an umbrella! The umbrella's shape collects the sound waves and reflects them back to the microphone.

To play a phonograph recording, the cylinder was rotated underneath the needle. The pattern of bumps and dips in the cylinder grooves vibrated the needle, which the drumhead and sound horn then turned back into sound waves.

### You will need

| | |
|---|---|
| a tape recorder | blank cassette tapes |
| a microphone | earphones |
| tape | an umbrella |
| three or four friends who will sing | |

*The very first phonograph recording was made in 1877 by the American inventor Thomas Edison.*

**1** Begin by lining your friends up in a row. Stand facing them with the microphone, and ask them to sing a song together. The tape will pick up the voice nearest the microphone, drowning out the rest.

**2** Now tape the microphone to the handle of an umbrella as shown above. Try to make the same recording again, standing in exactly the same place. Are the four voices more evenly balanced when you play back the tape?

**3** Take your equipment outside. Listen for birds singing, and then try to record them by pointing the microphone in their direction. The tape will pick up very little.

**4** Now try recording the birds using the umbrella. The difference is quite amazing! You can make a collection of your recordings and keep a record of when and where you taped the different birds.

Bats have poor eyesight, but a very good sense of hearing. They can hear ultrasound – high-pitched sounds, way beyond the human hearing range. Bats can use ultrasound to find their way around the dark caves they live in. When a bat makes a high-pitched squeak, the sound bounces off the wall of the cave and returns to the bat as an ultrasound echo. From the amount of time between the squeak and echo, the bat can tell how far away the wall is.

**1** Take a rectangle of black poster board, fold it over and draw the shape of a bat as shown above. Cut out this shape, unfold the card and you'll have a symmetrical bat. Make twelve bats, three for each player.

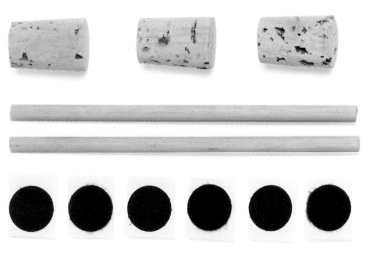

**2** Stick a hook-and-loop fastener dot to the wide end of each cork, and then glue the side of the cork to the bat's body to make a kind of pedestal for each bat.

### MAKE it WORK!
Make this batty ultrasound game! The playing board is a dark cave, criss-crossed by sound waves. The playing pieces are bats that cross the cave on the sound waves.

### You will need
pennies or buttons for scoring counters
dots made of hook-and-loop fasteners, or paper clips
thick and thin colored poster board
several wooden dowels
a toothpick
12 corks
glue

**3** If you don't have hook-and-loop fasteners or corks, simply attach a paper clip to the bottom of each bat as shown on the left. Hook-and-loop bats will sit on top of the sound waves. Paper clip bats, on the other hand, will hang below the sound waves.

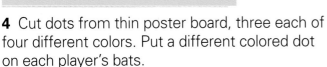
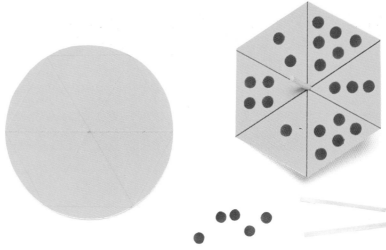

**4** Cut dots from thin poster board, three each of four different colors. Put a different colored dot on each player's bats.

**5** Make the spinner. Draw a circle and divide it into six segments. Snip off the sides to make a hexagon, and draw dots in each segement as shown.

**6** Poke a toothpick through the middle of the spinner. Twirl it around and it will come to rest on one of the six sides.

 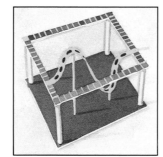

Assembling the board

**7** Now make the board. Cut a large square of thick poster board for the base. Cut four equal lengths of dowel and glue one upright in each corner.

**8** Cut four strips of thick poster board, each as long as a side of the base board. Divide each strip into sixteen small squares. Glue these strips in place on the wooden dowels, as shown in the diagram above.

**9** At each corner of the raised section put a square of paper in one of the players' colors.

**10** Cut six long strips of thin poster board to represent sound waves. If you have made hook-and-loop fastener bats, mark off the sound waves with hook-and-loop fastener spots. If you have paper-clip bats, stick a row of colored-paper spots on each sound wave.

**11** Put the sound waves in position, stretching the strips of thin poster board in wavy lines across the board from one raised side to the other. In some places, you will have to add extra dowel supports to hold up the sound waves and help them keep their shape.

## Playing the ultrasound game

In this game, each player has three bats which set off from the corner marked in their color. The aim of the game is to make as many flights as possible from one side of the board to the other within a set time limit.

**1** Decide on your time limit for the game – say fifteen or thirty minutes.

**2** Spin the spinner. The player with the highest number starts, and play passes to the left.

**3** The first player spins and moves a bat the corresponding number of spaces along the edge of the playing board. When a bat lands on a sound wave, it may cross the cave, spot by spot.

**4** Each time a bat completes a crossing, the player puts a scoring counter in his or her corner of the cave. The bat continues around the edge of the board until it reaches another sound wave.

**5** Players may use a spin to move any one of their bats. They may also split the score and move more than one bat.

**6** When two players' bats going in opposite directions meet, they cannot pass one another. The two players both spin the spinner. The bat with the higher score continues its flight with a new spin, but the lower-scoring bat falls off and goes back to its corner.

**7** At the end of the agreed time limit, the players have a race back to their corners, completing any waves they have already started. The first player to bring all three bats home gets three extra counters.

**8** The winner is the player who has collected the most counters.

Radio transmitters send sounds around the world, by changing sounds into electrical impulses and then **radio waves**. These waves of energy travel at the speed of light through air, solid objects, and empty space. Radio receivers pick up the waves and turn them back into sounds again.

## MAKE it WORK!

Make your own simple radio receiver and try tuning into radio signals. Remember that the signals will be weaker than a normal radio.

**Warning:** This crystal radio does not need a power supply and must NEVER be connected to an electrical outlet.

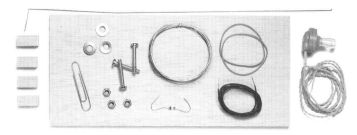

## You will need

| | |
|---|---|
| two rubber bands | thick balsa wood |
| an awl | 16 in. steel wire |
| wood glue | a large metal paper clip |
| paint | a germanium diode, |
| a sharp craft knife | and a crystal earpiece |
| wire strippers | from a hobby shop |

22 ft. bare (non-insulated, non-lacquered) copper wire
a cardboard tube, 9 in. long
three nuts, bolts, and washers
33 ft. single-strand insulated electrical wire

**1** Ask an adult to help you to cut a 9 in. x 4 in. piece of balsa wood for the base. Cut out four balsa wood feet and glue them to the corners.

**2** Make two supports for the tube, by cutting out semicircles from the balsa wood. Glue into position on the base. Paint the wood.

**3** Use the awl to make three small holes along the front of the base at **a**, **b**, and **c**. Put a washer over each hole. Push the bolts into the base and fix them under the board with nuts.

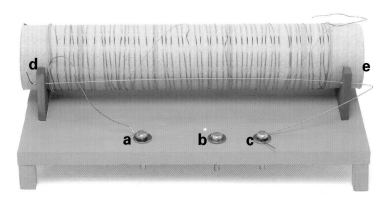

**4** Take the bare copper wire and leaving one short end free at **e**, carefully wind the rest around the cardboard tube. The coils **must not** touch each other.

**5** Secure the copper wire with rubber bands at both ends of the tube. Then wrap the long end of the copper wire around the bolt at **a**.

**6** Push the steel wire through the balsa wood supports in front of the copper coil, from **d** to **e**. Leave a short end at **d**, pushing it upward to secure. Bend the long end at **e** forward and wrap it around the bolt at **c**.

▲ The **diode** detects radio waves picked up by the **antenna** so that you can hear sounds in the earpiece.

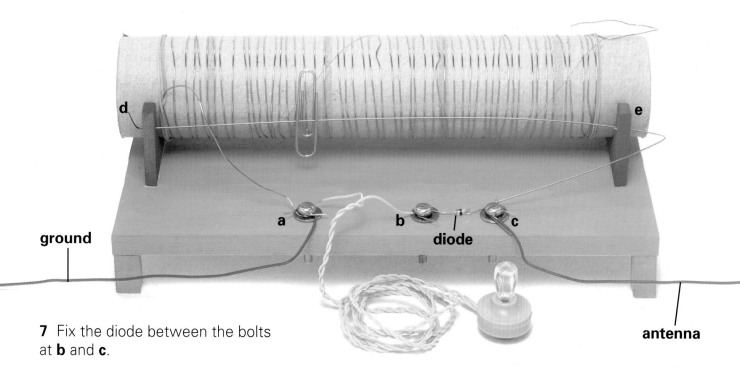

**ground**

**a**    **b**    **diode**    **c**

**d**    **e**

**antenna**

**7** Fix the diode between the bolts at **b** and **c**.

**8** Strip the insulation from the ends of both earpiece leads, using the wire strippers. Attach one end to the bolt at **a**, so that it touches the wire. Wrap the other end around the bolt at **b**.

**9** To make an antenna, cut 30 ft. of insulated wire. Strip off the insulation at one end of the wire and tie it around the bolt at **c**. Tie the other end to a post or tree in an outside space.

**10** To ground the radio, take 3 ft. of insulated wire and strip the covering from both ends. Attach one end to the bolt at **a**, and the other to a metal object, such as a clean, unpainted metal railing.

## NOTE
1. Keep surfaces of all connections clean.
2. Make sure all connections touch in the correct places, and nowhere else.
3. If you use lacquered copper wire, you must sandpaper the ends where they wrap around the bolts, and where the paper clip touches the copper wire.
4. Weather and location may affect reception. Your receiver will probably work best in a large open space away from tall buildings.
5. Try using different objects as antennas, and to ground your radio.

▼ To operate the radio, put in the earpiece and slip a metal paper clip onto the steel wire between **d** and **e**. Twist it backward, and move it slowly along the copper coil. You should hear faint clicks or a radio station. What the radio picks up depends on the number of turns of copper wire.

Every sound has its own pitch – high or low – depending on the shape of the sound wave. To a musician, each different pitch of sound makes an individual musical **note**.

Musical notes can be arranged in a special pattern called a **scale**. There are many kinds of scales, but the most common is called an **octave**. It is made up of eight notes that move higher and lower step by step. The notes on a piano are set out in octaves – and you might have sung the notes of an octave yourself: do, re, mi, fa, so, la, ti, do.

## MAKE it WORK!

Make your own instruments that play the notes of the octave scale. You will need to learn the notes of the octave, or copy them from a musical instrument – an instrument with fixed notes, such as a piano or electric organ, is easiest. If you don't play an instrument yourself, you could ask for some help from a friend or adult who does.

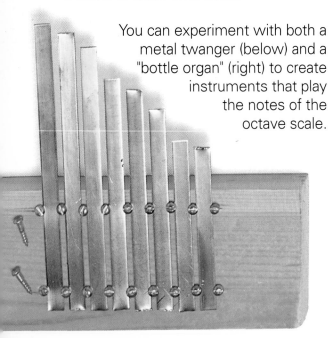

You can experiment with both a metal twanger (below) and a "bottle organ" (right) to create instruments that play the notes of the octave scale.

## For the "bottle organ" you will need

food coloring          a long nail
a musical instrument    water
eight bottles of the same size and shape

**1** Collect eight identical bottles and set them up in a line. (Milk bottles are probably the easiest to use.) Hit each bottle with a long nail. They should all make the same sound.

**2** Take a jug of water and pour a little into the first bottle. If you are going to copy a scale from a musical instrument, play the first note of the scale. Then gently hit the top of the bottle with the nail to see if it sounds close to the note you have just played. Gradually adjust the water level in the bottle until both bottle and instrument give out exactly the same note.

**3** Follow the same method for each bottle until you have made a complete octave.

**4** When you are happy with the sound of the "bottle organ," dye the water in each bottle with a few drops of food coloring. You will be able to see the different notes more easily.

**5** Now try to pick out a tune – something simple, such as "Twinkle, Twinkle, Little Star."

## Making a "metal twanger"

You can make another octave scale using strips of brass (previous page) or thick steel wire (right) fixed to a solid block of wood.

## For a "brass twanger" you will need

a small block of wood          a file
a thin strip of brass          screws
a small hacksaw                a screwdriver
a bradawl                      a hammer

**Be careful!** To make a "twanger," you will have to use sharp tools. Ask an adult to help you.

**1** Cut a short strip of brass and hold it in place on the block of wood. Pluck the end of the strip, and it will make a twanging noise.

**2** Now cut seven other strips of brass, each slightly longer than the last. Experiment with different lengths until you can arrange the strips on the block of wood to make an octave.

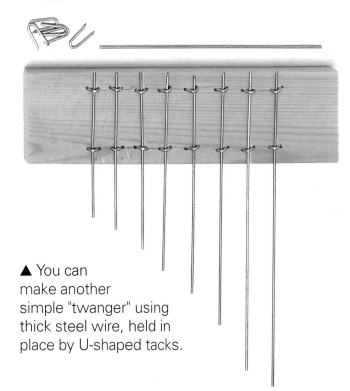

▲ You can make another simple "twanger" using thick steel wire, held in place by U-shaped tacks.

**3** File the sharp edges off the strips of brass and fix them in place. Mark where the screws should go with a bradawl, and then twist them into the wood with the screwdriver.

▼ Musicians check the pitch of an instrument with a tuning fork. When the fork is struck, its prongs vibrate at a regular speed, sending out a clear, single note that never changes.

*A lot of the pop music and classical music we hear is based on the eight-note scale, but some cultures use totally different scales. Much Chinese music is based on a sequence of five notes; Indian classical music often uses a twenty-two note scale.*

How many kinds of musical instruments can you think of? They come in many different shapes and sizes, from guitar to piano, synthesizer to tom-tom drums. Yet they all have one thing in common – they create sounds by making air vibrate.

### Musical pipes
Many musical instruments have pipes. Inside each pipe is a column of air. When this air is made to vibrate in a certain way, the pipe plays a note.

### MAKE it WORK!
Make your own music using pipe instruments. Panpipes are a set of pipes of different lengths, each of which makes a different note. Tubular bells are metal pipes that hang free and make a bell-like sound when hit with a large nail.

### To make the panpipes
**1** Have an adult help you use the utility knife to cut eight straws or eight pieces of plastic tubing in different lengths. Tape them together, stepped at one end, as shown at the right.

**2** To play the panpipes, blow gently across the top of each pipe at the end that is secured with tape to produce a note. You will find that longer pipes play a lower note than shorter pipes.

### You will need
glue
wood
copper pipe
nylon fishing line
flexible plastic tubing      tape
screws and a screwdriver      utility knife
plastic drinking straws      a hacksaw
                             a large nail

**3** Experiment with the lengths of the pipes. Can you make octave scales like those on the previous page?

## To make the tubular bells

**1** Ask an adult to help you cut eight pieces of copper pipe. Each one should be a little longer than the one before, so that you can arrange them in a stepped pattern.

**4** Hang the copper pipes from the top piece of the frame using pieces of strong fishing line. Thread the line through the holes you have drilled, and attach it to the copper pipes with tape.

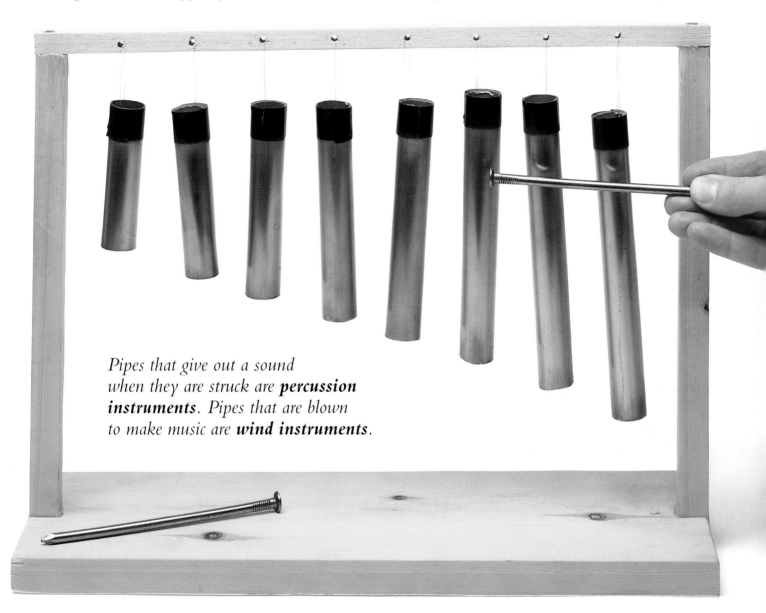

*Pipes that give out a sound when they are struck are* **percussion instruments**. *Pipes that are blown to make music are* **wind instruments**.

**2** Make a wooden frame. It should be big enough to hold the copper pipes hanging at well-spaced intervals. You will need a flat base, two side pieces and a top piece.

**3** Drill eight holes at equal spaces through the top piece of the frame. Then put the frame together, cutting the side supports into the baseboard. Glue the joints and secure them firmly with screws.

**5** Arrange the pipes in order of length. Strike them with a metal nail to make them chime.

Because the pipes hang free, they continue to vibrate after they have been hit, and thus, the sound lingers on. Try striking a pipe and then grasping the pipe tightly with your hand. The sound dies right away. As soon as you stop the pipe from vibrating, the sound waves stop being produced too.

Unlike our panpipes, many instruments create sounds by vibrating the air in just a single pipe. In these instruments, the different notes are made by altering the length of the main pipe. Recorders have holes to let the air out in different places. A brass trombone has a slide that moves up and down to change its length.

**1** Take a piece of copper pipe or a section of cardboard tubing. Leave a space at one end, and then use a bradawl to mark out evenly spaced holes along the rest of the pipe.

**2** Ask an adult to drill the holes you have marked. At the end of the pipe nearest the mouthpiece, cut a blowhole, following the diagram on the right.

▼ metal recorder

▼ brass-pipe recorder

▼ cardboard-tube recorder

▲ ▼ slide whistles

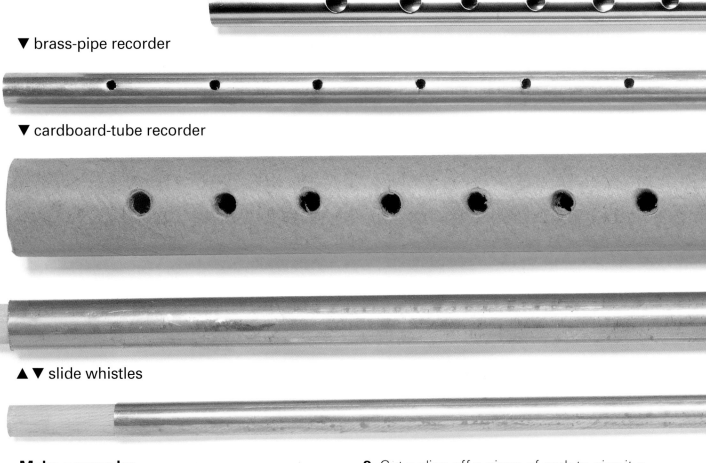

### Make a recorder

A recorder player sounds different notes by putting fingers over the holes to make the air travel different distances down the pipe.

### To make a recorder you will need

a tube of thick cardboard or copper pipe
a bradawl, drill and hacksaw
a cork

**3** Cut a slice off a piece of cork to give it a flat edge. Then sandpaper the cork to make it smooth and fit snugly inside the top of the recorder pipe. Position the flat side face up, opposite the blowhole and finger holes.

**4** Now blow gently into the mouthpiece. The cork and the blowhole are shaped so that the air inside the recorder is vibrated.

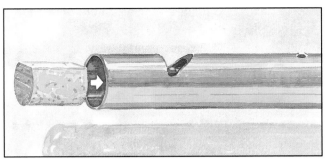

Making the recorder mouthpiece

## To make a slide whistle you will need

a copper pipe          tape or glue
wooden dowel
the mouthpiece from a party blower

**1** Ask an adult to cut a piece of pipe.

**2** Cut a piece of dowel about 6 inches longer than the pipe. The dowel should fit inside the pipe as tightly as possible, while still being able to move easily.

**3** Fit the party blower mouthpiece to one end, using glue or tape. If you cannot find a mouthpiece that fits, you can still play the slide whistle by blowing across the top of the pipe.

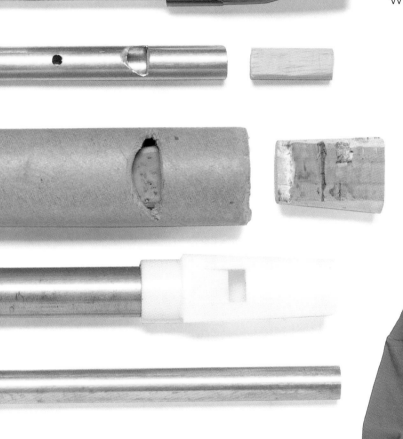

## Make a side whistle

Slide whistles make a weird wailing sound. The length of the pipe is changed by pushing a dowel in and out. There are no separate notes, just a continuous rising and falling tone.

*The width of a pipe, as well as its length, will affect the sound it makes. Narrow pipes make higher-pitched notes than wide pipes.*

Shakers and rattles are percussion instruments. They are often used to stress the rhythm of a piece of music and give it a strong beat. Shakers, like our paper cup shakers, make the air vibrate by moving loose objects inside an enclosed space. Rasps and rattles rub two rough surfaces together to make sound vibrations.

## To make the shakers you will need
paper cups                     tape
plastic bottles with lids
rice, lentils, chickpeas, beads and pebbles

**1** To make a paper cup shaker, put a handful of rice or lentils into one cup. Turn another cup upside down and tape the two cups together, rim to rim.

**2** To make plastic bottle shakers, simply pour a handful of beads or chickpeas into the bottle, and put the lid on tight. You could decorate the shakers with colored paper if you wish.

**3** Try making shakers with different-sized bottles. You will find that larger bottles which hold more air make deeper sounds.

## MAKE it WORK!
Make your own collection of different shakers and rattles. They can make a variety of sounds, depending on the amount of air each one vibrates and the kinds of surfaces that are rubbed up against one another.

▲ Experiment with different fillings for your shakers. You will find that paper cup shakers with lentils make a softer sound than plastic bottles with chickpeas.

## To make a rattle you will need
| | |
|---|---|
| a wooden dowel or stick | a hammer |
| several long, thin nails | enamel paints |
| metal bottle tops | a larger nail |

**1** Punch a small hole in the middle of each bottle top using the hammer and larger nail. **Be careful** as you do this! Put a piece of old wood underneath the bottle top, and don't hit your fingers.

**2** Slip four bottle tops onto each thin nail. (If you like, paint them first.) Then hammer the nails into the dowel or stick, making sure the tops can rattle freely, and that they don't slip off the ends of the nails.

## To make a sandpaper rasp you will need
| | |
|---|---|
| two blocks of wood | thumbtacks |
| two sheets of sandpaper | |

**1** Tack the sandpaper to the blocks of wood as shown below.

**2** To play the rasp, rub the two sandpaper surfaces together. It makes a soft, grating noise.

## To make a wooden rasp you will need
| | |
|---|---|
| a block of soft wood | a large nail |
| a small hacksaw | |

**1** Ask an adult to help you cut a zig-zag shape along the top of the block of wood as shown.

**2** To play the wooden rasp, run the nail back and forth along the uneven surface. It makes a harsher sound than the sandpaper rasp.

Both of these rasps make soft noises. Unlike the shakers, they have no space inside them where the air can vibrate to make the sounds louder.

Drums are probably the oldest and simplest musical instruments in the world. They contain a space filled with air, and have a flexible drumhead stretched across one end. When the drumhead is struck, it vibrates and makes a noise.

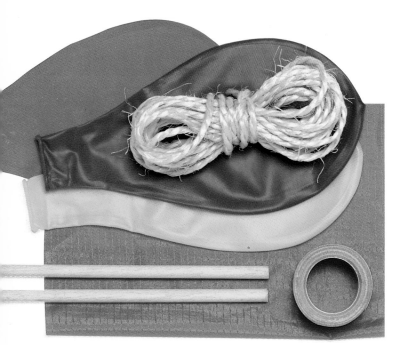

Although all drums work in basically the same way, they are able to make a range of different noises. Size is important. A big bass drum makes a much deeper sound than a small bongo drum. The drum's pitch is also affected by the drumhead. A tight drumhead makes a higher note than a slack one.

## MAKE it WORK!

Experiment with the sounds and tones of different drums. Try out some of these ideas and, if you like, put together a collection of drums to make your own drum kit.

## You will need

| | |
|---|---|
| balloons | thick paper |
| string | rubber bands |
| glue or tape | thin wooden dowels |

boxes and tin cans of all shapes and sizes
a sheet of plastic or an old plastic bag
an eyelet punch or cardboard hole reinforcers

### ▶ Bongo drums

**1** Cut cardboard tubes into several different lengths, to make bongo drums that will sound different notes.

**2** Cut flat pieces of balloon rubber to make the drumheads, and secure them across the tops of the cardboard tubes with elastic bands.

**3** Attach a dowel to each drum. That way you can hang them up, and the notes will sound more clearly from the open ends of the drums.

### ▲ Tin can drums

**1** Take the top and bottom off a tin can. Wash the can, being very careful not to cut yourself on any sharp edges inside.

**2** Stretch balloon rubber over the ends of the can, and secure it with elastic bands.

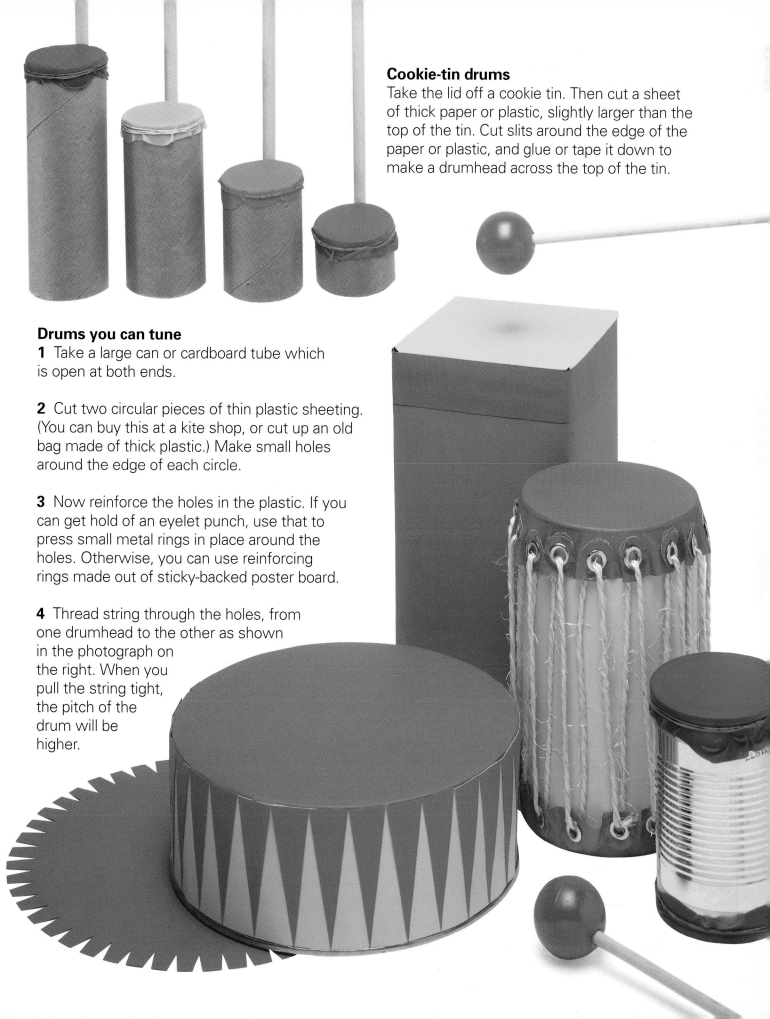

## Cookie-tin drums

Take the lid off a cookie tin. Then cut a sheet of thick paper or plastic, slightly larger than the top of the tin. Cut slits around the edge of the paper or plastic, and glue or tape it down to make a drumhead across the top of the tin.

## Drums you can tune

**1** Take a large can or cardboard tube which is open at both ends.

**2** Cut two circular pieces of thin plastic sheeting. (You can buy this at a kite shop, or cut up an old bag made of thick plastic.) Make small holes around the edge of each circle.

**3** Now reinforce the holes in the plastic. If you can get hold of an eyelet punch, use that to press small metal rings in place around the holes. Otherwise, you can use reinforcing rings made out of sticky-backed poster board.

**4** Thread string through the holes, from one drumhead to the other as shown in the photograph on the right. When you pull the string tight, the pitch of the drum will be higher.

In England whirling rattles like the one on this page were a common sight at soccer games. Fans on the sidelines would wave their rattles to cheer their team on.

Our rattle makes a very loud noise. It creates sound in two different ways. The wooden surfaces of the cog and tongue make a clattering noise as they hit one another, while the whirling movement of the rattle sets off its own rhythmic pattern of sound vibrations in the air around it.

## You will need

four metal washers
a drill and hacksaw
thin wooden dowel
thick wooden dowel
a fairly thick piece of wood about 1/4 in. thick for the frame of the rattle
thinner wood for the tongue of the rattle
matchsticks or thin slivers of wood
a thread spool
strong wood glue

**Be careful!** This project involves difficult woodworking. Ask an adult to help you with all the stages when you have to cut the wood or drill holes.

## MAKE it WORK!

Make your own whirling rattle, take it out of doors and see how loud a noise you can make with it!

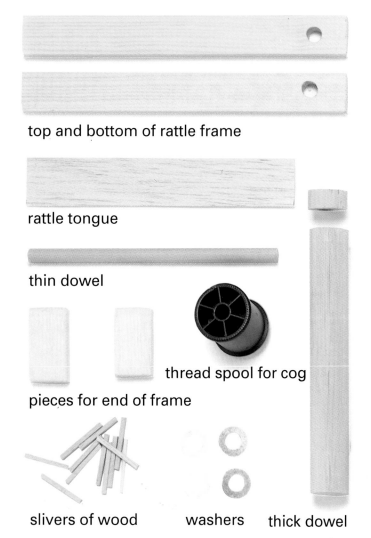

top and bottom of rattle frame

rattle tongue

thin dowel

pieces for end of frame

thread spool for cog

slivers of wood          washers          thick dowel

**1** Cut two identical rectangular pieces of the thicker wood. These will form the top and bottom of the frame of the rattle.

**2** Cut a rectangle of thin wood, slightly shorter than the width of the frame. This will be the tongue of the rattle.

**3** Cut the thick dowel in two – you need a long piece for the handle of the rattle, and a much shorter piece for the top.

**4** Cut two small rectangles of thick wood. They fit across the outer end of the rattle, with the tongue sandwiched between them.

**5** Make the cog wheel. Cut several thin slivers of wood, or cut the heads off several matchsticks. Then glue these sticks around the side of the spool, using strong wood glue.

**6** Take a drill the same width as the thin wooden dowel. Drill a hole through one end of the top and bottom pieces of the frame. Then drill the same size holes into the center of both pieces of thick wooden dowel.

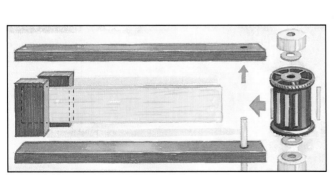

Assembling the whirling rattle

**Be careful!** Make sure that you use very strong wood glue to stick the pieces of the rattle together. Follow the instructions on the package carefully, and try not to let the glue touch your skin.

**7** Assemble the rattle as shown in the drawing below. Thread the thin dowel through the cog and slip a washer on either side. Then add the top and bottom of the frame, followed by two more washers. Fit the ends of the thin dowel into the holes you have drilled in the thicker dowel.

**8** Now glue the tongue and the outer end of the rattle in place. You must position the tongue very carefully. It should just touch the cog, so that it makes a noise, but should still be springy enough to let the cog spin around freely.

The washers in the whirling rattle reduce the friction between the pieces of wood and help the rattle swing more easily.

Have you ever burst a balloon by accident? The loud, unexpected bang can make you almost jump out of your skin! The air trapped inside the balloon suddenly rushes out, creating sound waves which we hear as a loud bang. The sound of any explosion is caused by air moving at great speed – that's why the blast from a bomb will knock over people and even buildings.

## MAKE it WORK!

Moving air will make all sorts of noises. It can hum, whistle and whir, as well as bang. Put together these simple cardboard gadgets and see how they create sounds that crash like a thunder clap or hum like a bumble bee.

## You will need

| | |
|---|---|
| colored poster board | glue |
| brown wrapping paper | string |
| scissors or utility knife | a metal washer |

## Making a "banger"

**1** Cut a square of poster board.

**2** Cut another square of brown paper, slightly larger. Snip this square in half from corner to corner to make a triangle.

**3** Place the brown paper on top of the poster board as shown, and fold it where it overlaps. Glue paper and poster board along the overlaps.

**4** Fold both poster board and paper from corner to corner.

**5** To make a sound, hold the corner of the "banger" as shown on the left. Sharply fling it downward. The paper beak will flick out and make a bang.

## ▲ Making a "whirrer"

**1** Cut out the two cardboard shapes shown on the left, to make the wing and flapper sections. Slot them together.

**2** Pierce two holes in the wing as shown, and glue a small metal washer to the nose to weight it down. Thread about a yard of string through the two holes.

**3** Take the "whirrer" outside and spin it around your head. At first, the wing will just make a clattering noise, but as you speed up the sound will change to a high-pitched whir.

## ▼ Making a "spinner"

**1** Cut two hexagons of colored poster board. Make two small holes at the center, and four or five larger holes around the edges.

**2** Glue the hexagons together. Thread a piece of string through the center holes and tie the ends together.

**3** Twist the string around and around. Then pull it outward. As you pull, the string will keep on winding and unwinding itself and the spinner will keep on humming.

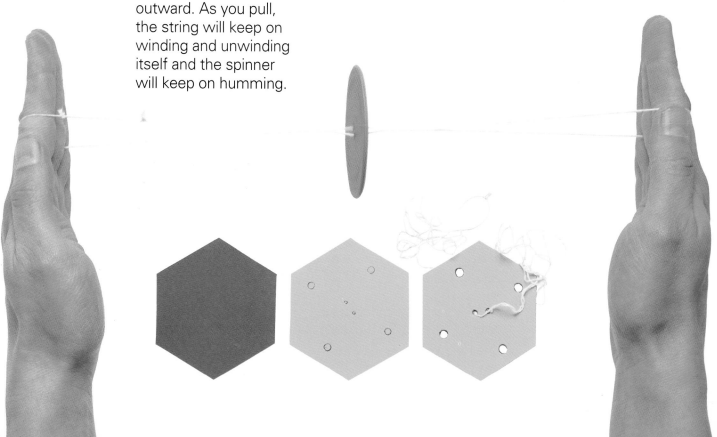

**String instruments** make music when a string or cord is plucked, so that the air around the string starts to vibrate. The pattern of a string instrument's sound waves depends on three things: the length of the string, what the string is made of and how tight it is.

A vibrating string on its own does not make much noise, so to make their sound louder, most string instruments have a **soundboard** and **resonator**. The soundboard picks up the strings' vibrations and transfers them to the resonator – a big space filled with air, which amplifies the sound.

## You will need

a wood box
a broom handle
a hammer
string
a drill
nails

## Make a wood box bass

Make your own instrument with one adjustable string and a wood box resonator.

**1** Ask an adult to help you drill a hole in one corner of the wood box. The broom handle should fit loosely inside the hole.

Drilling the hole

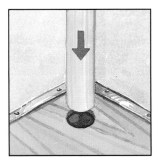
Fitting the handle

**2** Tap nails into the opposite corner of the wood box and the top of the broom handle. Tie a piece of string between the two nails.

**3** Put one foot on the box to hold it steady and pluck the string. Pull the handle back to tighten the string and make higher notes.
Push it forward for lower notes.

### Make a stretched-string zither
Each string on this zither is stretched by the weight of a water bottle so that it makes its own individual note.

### You will need
a hacksaw              a long wooden board
a metal strip          a hammer and nails
food coloring
eight bottles of the same size
eight equal lengths of string or fine twine

**1** Tap a row of eight nails into the middle of the wooden board. Space them out equally across the board.

**2** Ask an adult to help you cut a strip of metal the same width as the board. Make eight equally spaced grooves in the strip.

**3** Cut a groove across the wooden board, near one end, and wedge in the metal strip.

**4** Dye the pieces of string in eight different colors with food coloring. Fasten each string to a nail and run it across the metal strip and over the end of the board.

**5** Tie the loose end of each string tightly around the neck of a bottle. Then pour a different amount of water into each bottle. The more water in a bottle, the tighter the string will be, and the higher its note. Try to make an octave scale.

**6** Add food coloring to the water, to match the different strings.

## Playing strings

Many string instruments call for nimble fingers. Violinists or guitar players, for instance, hold down the strings in different places along the necks of their instruments. By altering the length of the strings they make different notes.

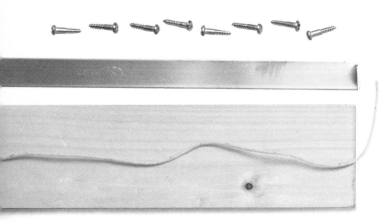

## Make a banjo

This home-made banjo is almost like the real thing. It has a bridge to transfer the strings' vibrations to the soundboard, and a large, plastic tub which acts as a resonator. See how many different notes it will play.

## You will need

a large, plastic tub
a strip of metal
wood, glue and string
a bradawl and hacksaw
a screwdriver and eight screws

**1** Cut a piece of wood for the soundboard. It's length should be about three times the width of the plastic tub.

**2** Ask an adult to cut four small grooves in the metal strip, to make a **bridge**. Then cut another groove across the soundboard, near the bottom, and glue the bridge in it.

**3** Mark holes in the wood where the screws will fit, following the photograph below. Twist the screws down a little way, and tie on the strings, leading them across the metal bridge.

**4** Ask an adult to cut another piece of wood, the same depth as the plastic tub, to support the soundboard. Glue this support and the soundboard in place.

**5** Twist the screws down farther in order to tighten up the strings and fine tune the banjo.

## Matchbox guitar

Stretch four rubber bands around a matchbox as shown on the left, and insert a bridge of thick poster board. The angle on the bridge means that each band is stretched by a different amount, so that it sounds a different note.

## Making guitars

Rubber band instruments are easy to make. Try either a large shoebox guitar, or the smaller, portable matchbox version.

## Shoebox guitar

To make the shoebox guitar, just cut a hole in the lid, and stretch the rubber bands across. Make the bridge from a sandwich of thick poster board and colored paper as shown below. It should be strong enough that you can slide it along to make the strings tighter.

### You will need

a shoebox
matchboxes
a utility knife or scissors
rubber bands of all sizes
thick poster board and colored paper

The shoebox guitar makes a deeper, richer sound than the little matchbox models, because the resonator is bigger and the strings (the rubber bands) are longer.

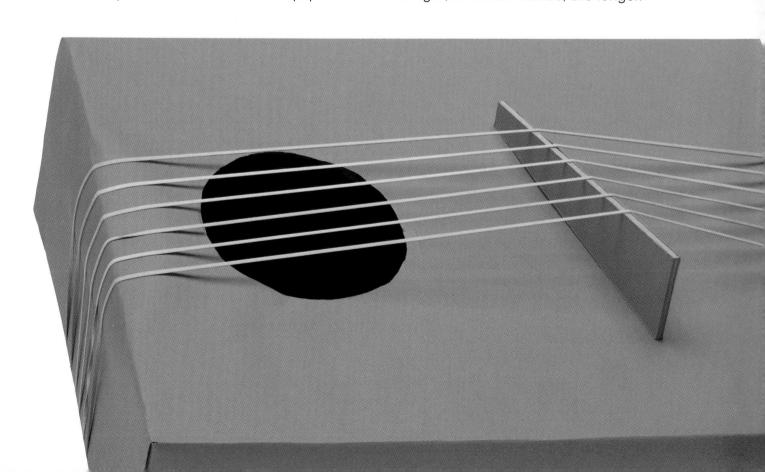

Nowadays, we can record music on cassettes or compact discs, but for hundreds of years, the only way of recording music was to write it down on paper. Over the centuries, a complicated system for writing music developed. This system of **musical notation** is now used for western music in many different countries.

The symbols and instructions on a **score** give all kinds of information to the musician – which notes to play and what rhythm to follow, how loud or soft, and how fast or slow the piece is. Learning to read and write music is like learning a new language.

▼ Western music is usually written on a set of five lines and four spaces called a **stave**. The positions of the notes on the stave tell the musicians which notes to play.

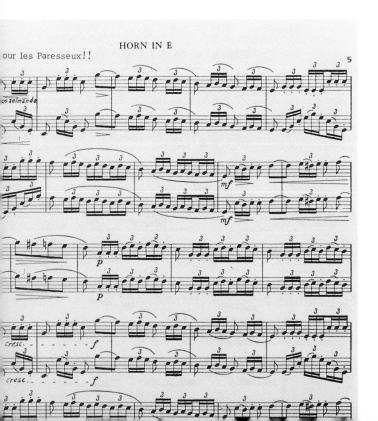

*Some of the instructions on a musical score – especially those about the speed of a piece – are usually written in Italian. Andante, for instance, means slowly. Prestissimo means as fast as you can.*

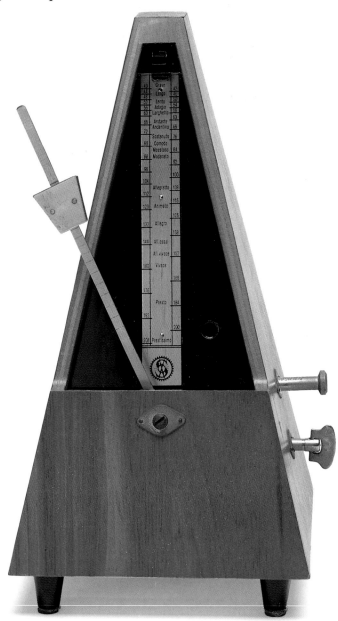

▲ To check that they are playing a piece at the right speed, musicians use a clockwork timer called a metronome. It has an upright pendulum that ticks backward and forward with a regular beat. By moving the weight up or down the pendulum, it can be made to tick more slowly or quickly.

## MAKE it WORK!

You can work out your own simple system of writing down music and use it to record any music you compose for your home-made instruments.

**1** Color in the stick-on spots to match the colors of the stretched-string zither on page 131 or the bottle organ on pages 116-117. The different colored spots will stand for the different notes.

**2** The size of the spots tells you how loudly to play the instrument. Small spots mean you play the note softly *(piano)*, medium-sized spots mean medium loud *(mezzo forte)* and large spots are loud *(forte)*.

**You will need**

graph paper
white spot stickers in three sizes

▶ Here's a simple example, going up the octave scale and down again, not too loud and not too soft.

▶ Up and down the scale again. Softly on the way up, loudly on the way down.

▶ Music for two players. The line stands for a drum beat every other note. The guitar plays orange and red notes, getting louder and louder.

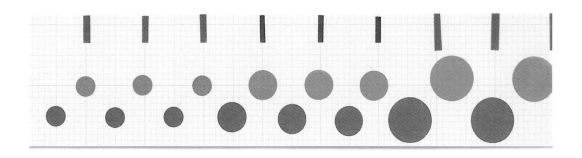

# Building

Bridges, towers, domes, dams, canals—these wonderful things are designed and built by engineers. The engineer's job is not easy: these structures must carry huge loads and last for many years, as well as look good.

## MAKE it WORK!

In this book you will learn how different structures are put together and why they are strong. You don't need to build a steel bridge to see why bridge **girders** should form triangles, because plastic straws work in just the same way. You will discover how a canal lock works, why an arched bridge is stronger than a flat one, and how to turn a flat sheet into a hollow dome.

To make a strong structure, whether it is a suspension bridge or a simple garden wall, you must understand the **forces** that will make it stay up. The key to success is in understanding how to choose the right **materials** and how to put them together correctly.

### You will need

You can build most of the projects found in this book out of simple materials, such as cardboard and wood, plastic straws, and other odds and ends. However, you will need some tools to cut, shape, and join all the different materials. All of the equipment above will be very useful as part of your engineer's tool kit.

## Planning and measuring

Always plan your projects carefully before you start to build. Measure each part accurately and mark it with a pencil before you begin to cut. Mark the positions of holes before you start drilling them. A plastic measuring cup will be helpful for the projects involving water.

## Safety!

Sharp tools are dangerous. Always be careful when you use them, and ask an adult to help you. Make sure that anything that you are cutting or drilling is held firmly so that it does not slip. If you can, borrow a small table vise. It will make drilling and sawing much safer.

## Cutting

You will need a saw for cutting wood and scissors for cutting cardboard and paper. A craft knife is useful too, but be extra careful with the sharp blade. Always cut away from your fingers. Use sandpaper or a file to round off any sharp edges.

## Joining

There are many ways to join the parts of your models together: a glue stick used with a glue gun is one of the easiest. Different kinds of fasteners, such as nails, nuts, bolts, and hook-and-loop fasteners, are described on page 141.

## Drilling

For some of the projects in this book, you will have to drill holes. Use a pointed awl to start the holes and then finish them off with a hand drill. This stops the drill from sliding.

The scientist Isaac Newton built a wooden bridge without using any screws, nails, or glue. After his death the bridge was taken apart for repairs, but no one could figure out how to put it back together! It was finally rebuilt with nuts and bolts.

## Push joints

Push joints are a simple way of joining materials. You can make a push joint between two plastic straws by putting glue on the end of one straw and pushing it into the end of another. Use pipe cleaners to join three or four straws, as shown in **a** below, but be careful of sharp ends. Plastic rods can be held tight with a push joint if you slide them into piping that has had a hole drilled through it, as in **b**.

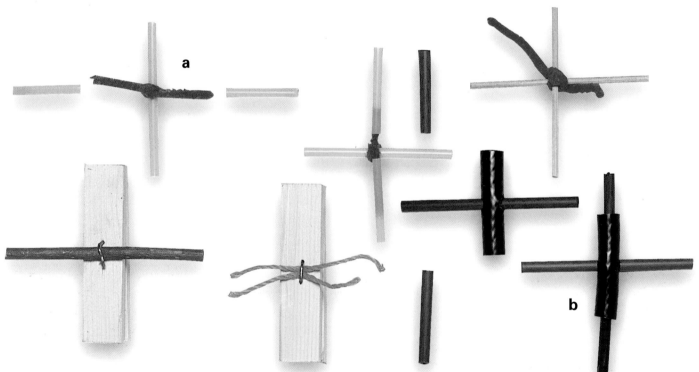

## MAKE it WORK!

Newton's bridge slotted together like a jigsaw puzzle. Usually builders need glue, screws, cement, or nails to make strong joints. Here are some ways you can make joints for your own projects.

## Staple joints

Use a hammer to tap a metal staple into a piece of wood to hold a rod or piece of cord in place. A staple gun is an excellent way of attaching cardboard to wood, but you should ask an adult to help you use it.

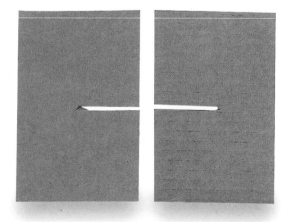

## Slot joints

The picture on the left shows how you can make slot joints. Cut slots in two pieces of cardboard and slide them over each other so that the pieces of cardboard cross at an angle.

## Glue joints

Glue from a glue gun is one of the quickest ways to join many items. However, be careful —the glue is very hot and you can easily burn your fingers. To make strong joints, the surfaces being glued together must be clean and dry. Use a piece of sandpaper to roughen them so that the glue can get a better grip.

## Gussets

Gussets are small pieces of a material, often metal, used to strengthen a joint. The gusset is attached across the joint. It increases the surface of the joint so that the force on it is spread out over a larger area. You can see below how you could use a cardboard gusset to strengthen a joint between two plastic straws.

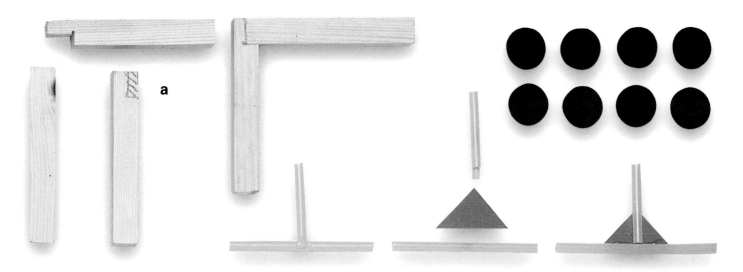

## Joining wood

Wood can be joined with nails, screws, or glue. If you use glue, you can make the joint much stronger by cutting slots in the wood, like the ones in **a** above. The glue then covers more of the surface of the wood than is possible when the pieces are stuck straight together.

## Hook-and-loop fasteners

Patches of hook-and-loop fasteners behave like bristly seeds that stick to your clothes. Each bristle on one side of the patch has a hook on the end which sticks to the side of the patch with furry loops. You can buy self-adhesive patches, or ones that you stick on with glue. Hook-and-loop fasteners will make joints that you can take apart and put back together again.

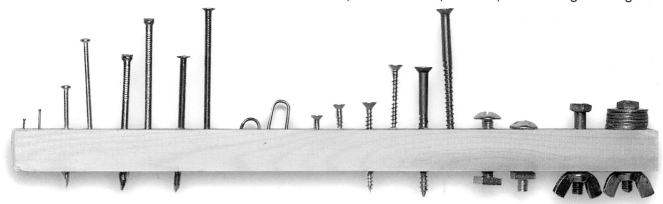

## Nuts, bolts, nails, and screws

These metal fasteners are an essential part of any builder's tool kit.

*A structure is no stronger than the joints between its parts. If the joints are weak, the structure will soon fall apart.*

It is possible to build a strong wall from stone or bricks without using cement or mortar. The wall is held together by the weight of the blocks or bricks pressing down on one another. Some very famous structures were built like this, including Stonehenge in England, the Egyptian pyramids, and Aztec temples in Mexico.

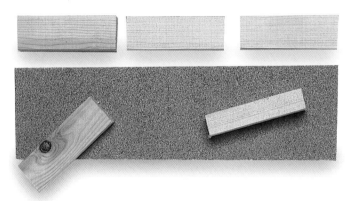

## MAKE it WORK!

The key to making a strong brick wall is the pattern in which the bricks are arranged. Build a number of walls with wooden bricks, using different patterns for the bricks. Which wall is the strongest?

**1** First make your bricks out of the balusters. They should be about 4½ in. long. Don't worry if your strip of wood isn't exactly the suggested dimensions—just make the bricks three times as long as they are wide. Measure and mark the wood with a ruler and pencil, then cut it carefully with a saw.

**2** Sandpaper the rough edges off your bricks.

**3** You are now ready to start building. First build a wall by piling the bricks one on top of another, with the gaps in one layer directly above the gaps in the layer beneath (see below, far left). This produces a weak wall that is easily demolished.

**4** Now stack the bricks as shown in the second wall from the left. This is much more effective. With this pattern, the gaps in neighboring layers of your wall do not line up. Each brick is holding the pair of bricks below it in place and is in turn held in place by the two bricks above.

**5** Double-skinned walls, like the two below on the right, are much stronger than walls built with a single thickness of bricks. The two sides of a double wall are linked by bricks turned through right angles, known as **headers**.

## You will need

| | |
|---|---|
| a pencil | a small saw |
| a ruler | sandpaper |

several narrow stair balusters, about ⅝ in. x 1½ in., found at builder's supply stores

The space or cavity in the middle of a wall of this type helps to keep a building warm, putting a protective air pocket between the inside and the outside. Sometimes the cavity is filled with foam for extra **insulation**.

# Trembling Tower

▲ A brick tower or chimney relies on the weight and pattern of its bricks to give it strength in much the same way as a brick wall. By experimenting with this tower, you will discover where the forces that keep the tower from toppling over are acting.

## How high can you build?

**1** Build a tower like the one shown above.

**2** Take bricks one at a time from the sides of the tower and place them on the top.

**3** How high can you build the tower before it collapses?

You will find that the bricks at the bottom of the tower are much more difficult to slide out than bricks higher up. This is because the weight of the bricks near the top of the tower **compresses** them. If you remove bricks from the bottom of the tower, the bricks above no longer have a firm base on which to rest, and so the tower falls over.

*The weight that presses down on the bricks at the base of a tall tower can be tremendous. The leaning tower at Pisa in Italy is falling over because its **foundation** was built on unstable soil.*

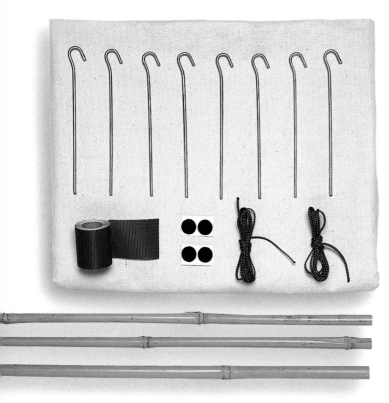

When you pitch a tent, it is kept in shape by the **tension** in the canvas and **guy ropes**. If you have a tent, you can set up house almost anywhere. Then, when you want to move on, you just release the tension, fold up the canvas, and pack it into your bag.

### MAKE it WORK!

When you stretch out a canvas tent and peg it down, tension is produced in the fabric. The upward push from the poles resists this tension. The balance of the forces pushing up and pulling down on the canvas gives the tent its rigid shape.

### You will need

| | |
|---|---|
| friends to help you | scissors |
| strong packing or mailing tape | tent stakes |
| a large cotton or canvas sheet | nylon cord |
| sticky-backed hook-and-loop fastener patches | |
| bamboo poles (one longer and two shorter than the sheet) | |

**1** The best place to pitch your tent is outside on some grass. Spread out the canvas sheet, making sure you have plenty of space around to stretch out the nylon guy ropes.

**2** On the outside of the sheet, reinforce the corners of the canvas with patches of tape. Turn the canvas over and place the long bamboo pole along the middle of the sheet to make the ridge of the tent.

**3** Tape the long pole in place. Using tape patches, reinforce both sides of the canvas along each edge, at the halfway point.

**4** Tie pieces of cord securely to the tops of the two shorter poles. Stick pieces of hook-and-loop fasteners on top of each short pole and on the underside of the ridge pole at each end.

**5** Ask your friends to attach the tent poles with the fasteners, and hold the tent up while you stake the canvas down.

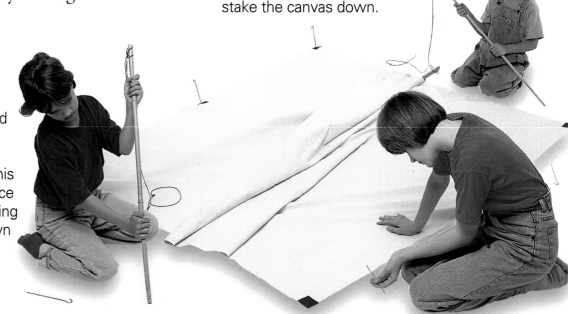

**6** Carefully stretch out the corners of the tent until it is taut, making sure that the lower edges still touch the ground. Push stakes into the grass through the four corner patches and then along the sides.

**7** Finally, stretch out the cords from the tops of the short poles to make guy ropes, and stake them firmly in place.

*Modern tents designed for expeditions are made with super-lightweight materials. A whole tent, including poles and stakes, may weigh only 2½ lbs., yet it can withstand a blizzard and keep the people inside warm and dry.*

Most tents need to be staked to the ground to stretch them into shape, but a hoop tent stands up without any stakes or guy ropes. Springy poles bent into hoops provide the tension needed to stretch the fabric.

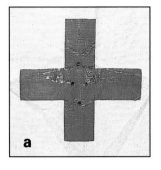

**a**   **b**

## You will need

| | |
|---|---|
| scissors | nylon cord |
| friends to help you | safety goggles |
| strong packing tape | awl |

six short, springy plastic poles
three long, springy plastic poles
a large square of canvas or cotton fabric
nine pieces of plastic tubing drilled with holes
 large enough to slide the poles through

**1** Spread the canvas on the floor and stick patches of tape on it at the 13 points shown.

**2** Using an awl, carefully make holes through the taped canvas 1¼ in. apart as shown in **a**, above.

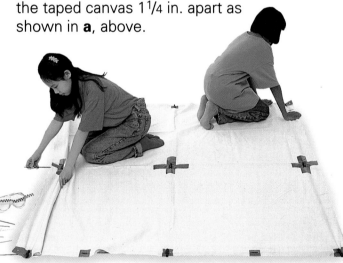

## MAKE it WORK!

The poles used for this tent are made from a very flexible plastic. You can buy them at a gardening supply store. Before modern plastics were invented, hoop tents were not common. Poles made from bamboo or metal will not bend far enough without breaking.

Make three holes in each corner patch of tape. Make four holes in the patches in the middle of each side and in the center of the canvas. In each of the remaining patches, make two holes parallel to the canvas edge.

**3** Place the long poles across the top, center, and bottom of the canvas. Position the six short poles in between to make four squares as shown at left.

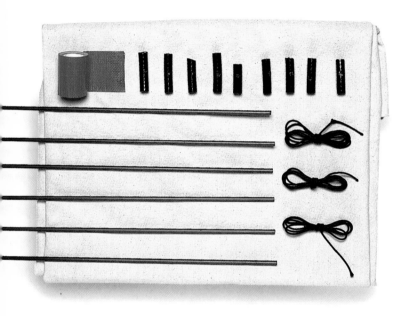

**5** Push pieces of tubing onto both ends of the long poles, as shown in **b**, at left. Now thread the short poles through the canvas and plug them into the open ends of the tubing.

**6** Turn the tent over and fasten each pole to the canvas with tape.

**7** Tie pieces of cord to the ends of the three poles sticking out from one edge of the fabric. Push the pole-ends into the ground.

**8** Wearing the goggles, bend the poles into hoops and push the free ends into the ground. Fasten the poles firmly in place with the cord. To make your tent extra secure, you could also use tent stakes to hold the canvas down.

**Note**
The poles and cords of the finished tent may need adjusting so that the tension in the canvas is even.

**4** Thread the long poles through the holes on one edge of the canvas to the holes halfway across. Push each pole through the drilled holes in a piece of tubing, then continue to thread the pole to the other side of the canvas.

Engineers build dams to stop the flow of water in a river. The water trapped by the dam forms a reservoir that can supply water to a city. The dam can also generate electricity for the city. Water from the reservoir flows through tunnels inside the dam, which contain turbines. The turbines are turned by the water flow and drive generators to create electricity.

### MAKE it WORK!

A dam must be strong enough to withstand the huge **pressure** of the water behind it. The deeper the water, the stronger the dam needs to be. What is the strongest shape for a dam? A flat wall, or a curve? Try some experiments to discover the answer.

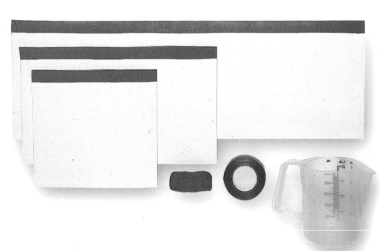

### You will need

| | |
|---|---|
| colored tape | scissors |
| a large fish tank | modeling clay |
| a measuring cup | thin cardboard |

**1** Cut out a rectangle of cardboard just a little wider than your tank.

**2** Cut thin strips of tape and stick them at equal distances above each other up one corner of the tank. This scale will measure the water level in the tank.

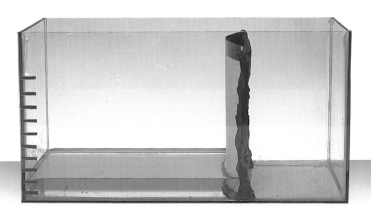

**3** To make the dam, attach the cardboard rectangle inside the tank by placing modeling clay along its sides and lower edge. Because the cardboard is slightly wider than the tank, it will curve when you fit it in place.

**4** Make sure that the clay seal is watertight all the way around the cardboard, or your dam will not work properly.

**5** Now use the measuring cup to pour water into the tank, making sure that the dam curves toward the section that contains the water.

**6** Keep filling the tank steadily, until the dam begins to leak. Make a note of the water level at this point, then continue pouring the water until the dam bursts.

How did your dam fail? Did the seal around the edges start leaking, or did the cardboard buckle and give way under the water pressure?

*People are not the only creatures to build dams. Beavers fell trees with their powerful teeth to block a stream. The lake formed behind the dam makes an excellent fishing ground for the beaver family.*

**7** Now make a dam using a rectangle of cardboard that is one and a half times the width of the tank. The cardboard will curve much more this time. Add water as you did in **6**. Which dam holds more water?

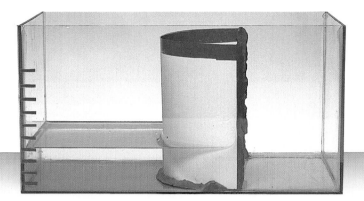

*The Grand Coulee Dam on the Columbia River in Washington is the biggest concrete dam in the world. It is 1 mile long.*

**8** Finally, make another dam with a length of cardboard two or three times the width of the tank. This will make a beautifully curved dam. Add water. How much water will this dam hold? It will probably be the strongest of the three.

Can you build a dam using other materials?

A dam wall gets its strength from its curved shape. The curve can withstand forces pressing on it that would burst a flat dam wall. The curve acts in the same way as the blocks of the **arched** bridge on pages 160-161. The more water that presses onto the dam, the tighter the blocks of the dam are squashed together.

Rivers flow downhill from their source to the sea. Where the ground slopes steeply, the water tumbles in rapids and falls. A canal lock slows the flow and holds the water between the lock gates, making it possible for a boat to pass safely up or down the water levels.

## MAKE it WORK!

This model lock works like a modern canal lock. The gates slide up and down like a guillotine. In a real lock, the gates are opened and shut by electric motors.

In England there are very old locks with hinged gates that are opened and closed by hand.

### You will need

a toy boat      gravel
modeling clay      four corks
a measuring cup
pieces of plywood
a long, narrow water tank
four grooved wooden strips, bought from a craft supply store (or eight short strips glued together in pairs)

**1** Stand the wooden strips upright inside the tank and attach them with the modeling clay as shown. If necessary, seal the edges of the lock with clay to make them watertight.

**2** Cover the bottom of the tank with gravel. Make the gravel layer thicker on one side of the lock than on the other to make different depths of water.

**3** Ask an adult to help you cut the lock gates from the plywood. The gates should slide smoothly up and down in the grooves of the strips. Drill a finger hole at the top of each gate and two holes for corks at the bottom.

**4** Fit corks into the lower holes and slide the gates shut.

**5** Now pour some water into the tank. Half fill the inside of the lock and the end with least gravel. Make the water level at the other end of the tank much deeper than this.

### Operating the lock

To operate the lock, first float a boat at the end of the tank with the lower water level, so that the boat can pass through into the lock. When the boat is inside, lower the lock gate. Now you must raise the water level in the lock so that the boat can float out to the upper level.

Remove one cork from the second gate, or lift the gate slightly. Add more water to the end section of your tank to simulate the water coming from upstream.

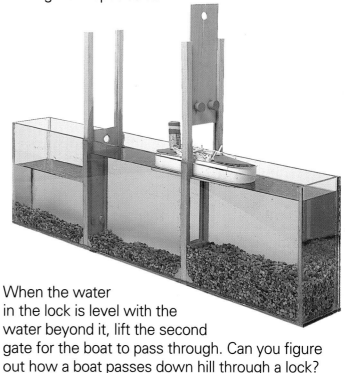

When the water in the lock is level with the water beyond it, lift the second gate for the boat to pass through. Can you figure out how a boat passes down hill through a lock?

Cable cars carry passengers high up into the mountains, where there are no roads or trains. The **gondolas**, or cars, hang from a huge loop of thick, steel rope strung between two towers. To take the weight, both the towers must be extremely strong. They also need to be set in firm foundations so that they do not topple over.

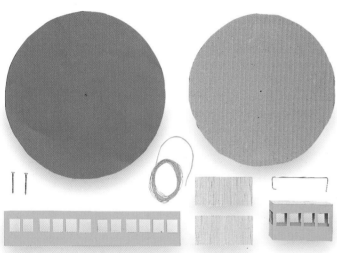

## MAKE it WORK!

Use your tower-making skills to build this model cable car. The gondolas run between towers made from strips of balsa wood. The strips are stuck together in triangles to give the towers the strength to carry the load.

### You will need

| | |
|---|---|
| two screws | string |
| strips of balsa wood | thin wire |
| thick corrugated cardboard | colored tape |
| thin cardboard and strong glue | modeling clay |

**1** Cut two rectangles of balsa wood to make the roof and floor of each gondola.

**2** Make the gondola walls from thin cardboard. Cut holes for the windows as shown.

**3** Assemble the gondolas. Glue the walls to the edges of the roof and floor. Tape a small piece of bent wire to the roof so that you can hang the gondola from the cable.

**4** Now build the towers. Arrange the balsawood strips in triangle shapes as shown. Make one tower two stories high, and the other four stories. Secure the joints with strong glue.

**5** Glue small cardboard gussets around the joints to strengthen them (see page 141).

**6** Cut squares of balsa to fit the tops of each tower and glue them in place. Strengthen them with a gusset at each corner (see page 141).

**7** To make the large wheels around which the cable turns, draw two circles on corrugated cardboard and cut them out. Then cut four slightly larger circles out of thin cardboard. Glue each small, thick circle between two large, thin ones.

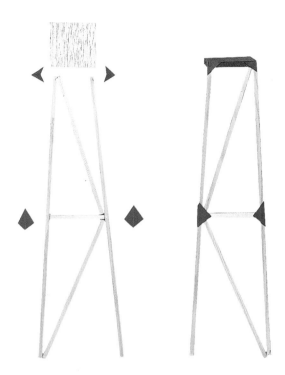

*The cables on a real cable car are kept slack so that there is as little tension in the cable as possible. If a cable were stretched too much, it would pull on the towers or run the risk of snapping in a strong gust of wind.*

▼ Turn one of the cable wheels to make the gondolas travel up and down between the towers.

**8** Make a hole in the center of each cable wheel. Push screws through the wheels and twist them into the balsa-wood squares on top of the towers. Make sure that the cable wheels turn freely on the screws.

**9** To keep the towers from toppling over, you must attach them to the floor or weight them down at the base with modeling clay. Real towers are set in massive concrete foundations.

**10** Loop the string around the wheels and tie the ends together. Do not pull the string too tight, or the tension will damage the towers.

**11** Hang the gondolas from the cable. Use a small piece of tape to keep them from sliding down the slope.

*A cable car moves when its operator pushes a lever that causes the car's heavy metal grip to latch onto the moving cable.*

Some shapes are naturally stronger than others. For instance, a square is very weak. A square frame, made from four pieces of wood nailed together, can easily be squashed into the shape of a diamond. Triangles are much stronger than this. Three pieces of wood joined together in a triangle are rigid and will not twist out of shape. When bridges and towers are built from tubes or girders, the parts are put together in triangles to give the structure strength.

**You will need**

an awl          a board
a vise and a drill     a tape measure
two pieces of strong nylon rope, about 5½ ft.
    and 4½ ft. long
three pieces of wooden broom handle, each
    about 3 ft. long

**1** Ask an adult to help you drill a hole about 1 in. from each end of each pole.

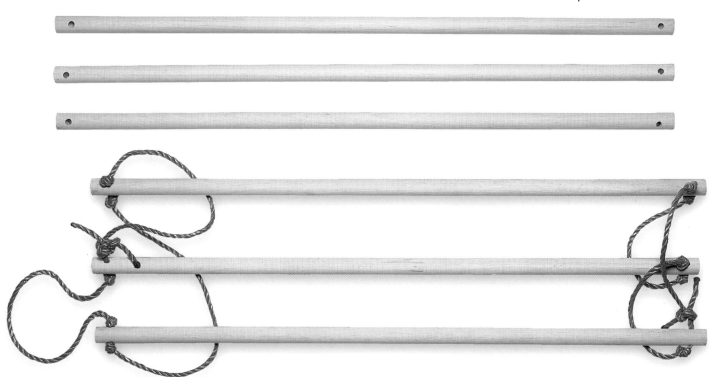

**MAKE it WORK!**
This stool is made from just three wooden poles and two pieces of rope. There are no nails or screws, yet it can hold the weight of a person. The stool gets its strength from its shape. The poles and ropes are arranged in triangles. These triangles fit together to make two rigid pyramids, one on top of the other.

**2** Now fasten the poles together with the ropes as shown. First tie a thick knot 4 in. from the end of one rope. Thread the long end of this rope through a hole in the first pole.

**3** Tie a second knot in the rope on the other side of the hole, so that the pole is held firmly between the two knots.

**4** Secure the second pole between two knots in the same way, leaving approximately 16-20 in. of rope between the poles.

**5** Leave free an identical length of rope and tie the third pole in place.

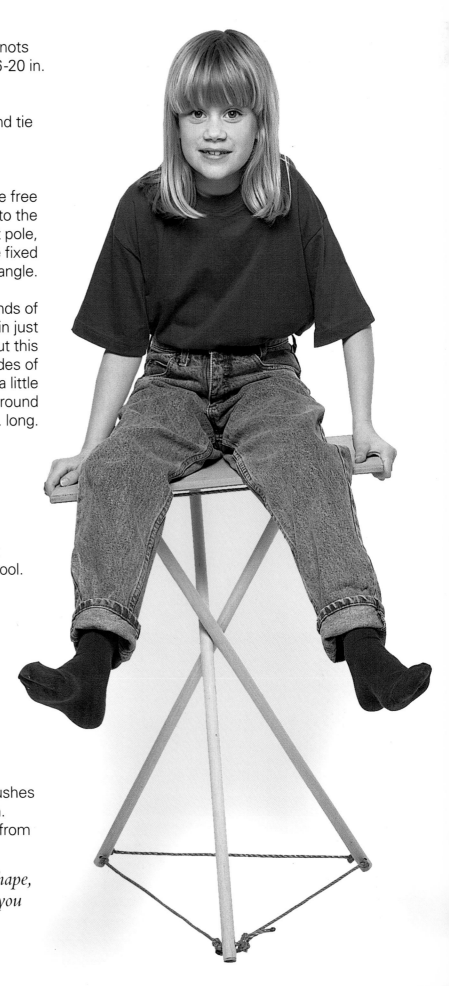

**6** Finally, tie the free end of rope back to the short end on the first pole, so the three poles are fixed in an equal-sided rope triangle.

**7** Now tie the other ends of the poles together in just the same way—but this time, make the sides of the triangle a little shorter: around 12-16 in. long.

### ▲ Setting up the stool

Once all three poles are roped together at both ends, you are ready to set up your stool. It can be tricky, so you'll probably need to ask a friend to help you.

Pull all three poles apart so that the rope triangles are stretched out. Stand the larger triangle on the floor, and then twist the smaller triangle around until all three poles cross in one place. Now rest a board on top and take a seat!

### Tension and compression

When you sit on the stool, your weight pushes down on the poles and compresses them. The tension in the ropes keeps the poles from sliding and keeps the stool rigid.

*A bicycle frame is built in a triangular shape, so that it does not twist or buckle when you put your weight on it.*

Have you seen a tower crane lifting girders high over the rooftops in the city or loading cargo onto the ships at the docks? The swinging **boom** on top of the tower moves the load carefully into position.

## You will need

| | |
|---|---|
| three empty thread spools | string |
| small plywood squares | gravel |
| pieces of dowel | |
| a yogurt cup with a string handle as shown | |
| thumbtacks | |
| paper clips | |
| a glue gun | |

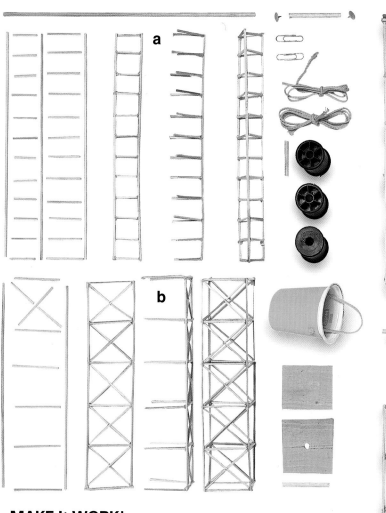

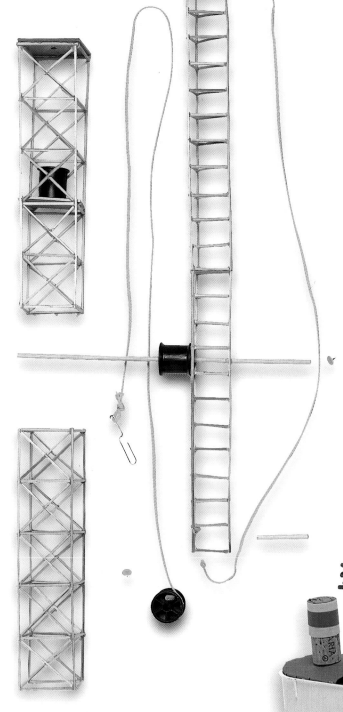

a

b

## MAKE it WORK!

A tower crane must be strong and light so that it is easy to move. The boom must also be well balanced so that the tower does not topple over when the crane lifts a load. The boom of this model crane is balanced with a yogurt cup that is filled with gravel. The crane is constructed from dowel girders arranged in triangles for strength. The girders of a real crane are made of steel.

**1** To make the three-sided boom, first glue dowel pieces 1¼ in. long between two dowel pieces 9½ in. long, to make a flat ladder (see **a** left).

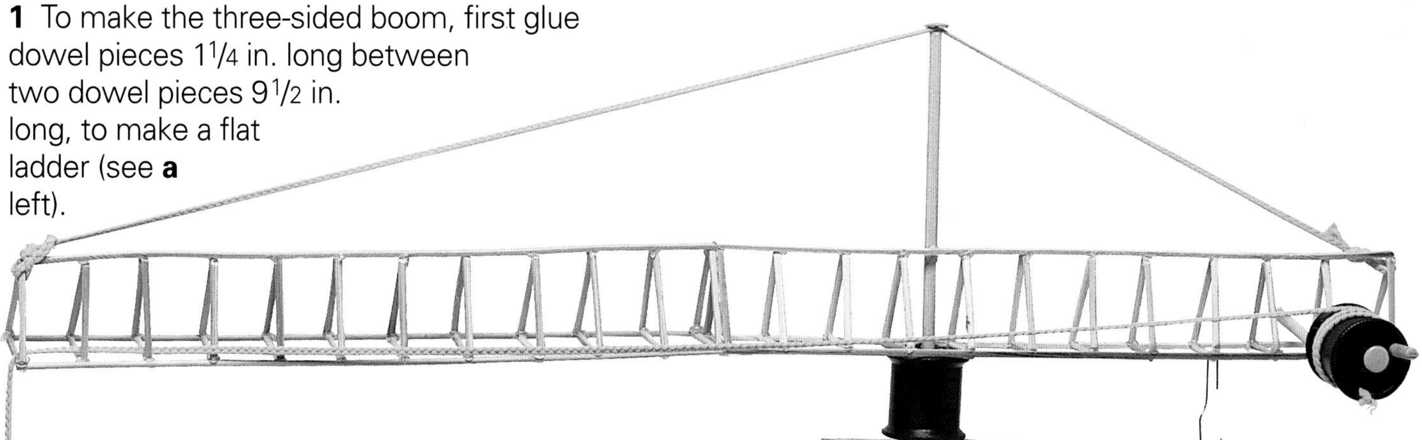

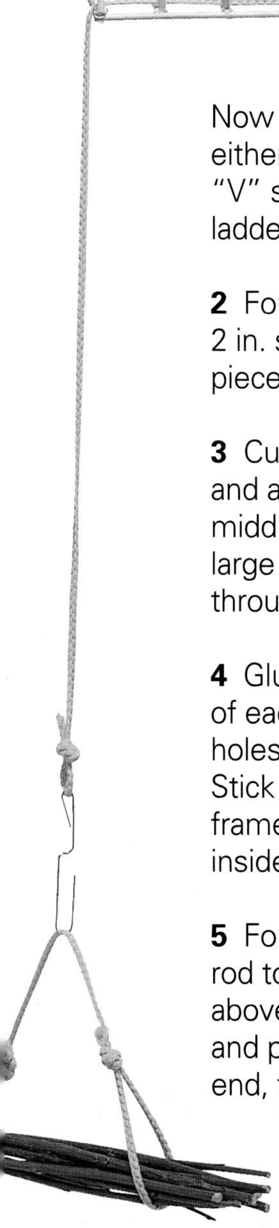

Now glue more short dowel pieces to either side of a third piece of dowel, in a "V" shape. Join this structure to the flat ladder to complete the boom.

**2** For the tower, make two box frames 2 in. square and 9¾ in. tall from dowel pieces (see **b** left).

**3** Cut a plywood square with 2-in. sides and another square a little smaller. In the middle of the 2-in. square, drill a hole large enough for a dowel rod to pass through.

**4** Glue a thread spool to the center of each square. Be sure to match the holes of the spool and the 2-in. square. Stick the 2-in. square on top of one box frame, then stick the smaller square inside the same frame (see right).

**5** For the **winch**, glue a short dowel rod to the end of the boom as shown above. Put a thread spool on the dowel and push a thumbtack into the dowel end, to hold the spool in place.

**6** Join the boom and tower with a piece of dowel as shown, then hang the yogurt cup from the boom as a **counterbalance**.

**7** Thread and fasten the strings as shown. Use a dowel to make a handle for the thread spool winch to lift the load.

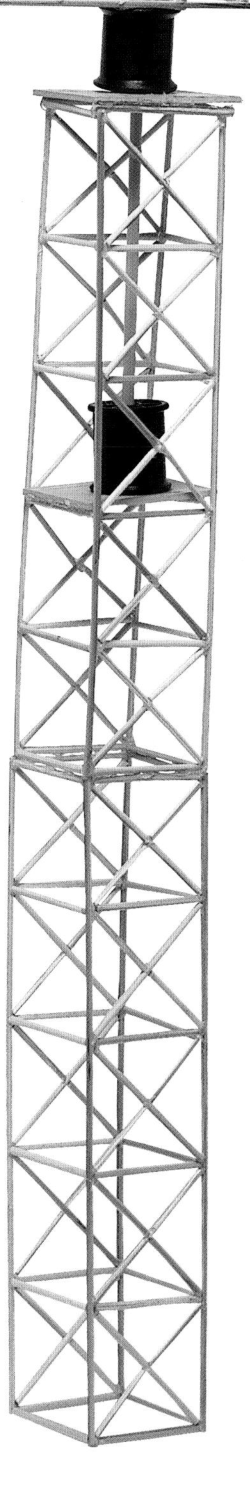

You will need to adjust the position of the counterbalance according to the size of the load. If the crane topples forward as it lifts the load, move the counterbalance back. In a real crane, the counterbalance adjusts itself automatically as the load is moved by the boom.

*A large tower crane can lift a load of about 30 tons to a height of 500 feet.*

Have you ever had to wait in traffic for a drawbridge to close? A drawbridge moves to allow tall ships to pass along a river or a canal. Some bridges, called swing bridges, swing sideways to open. Others, like the one shown here, move up and down.

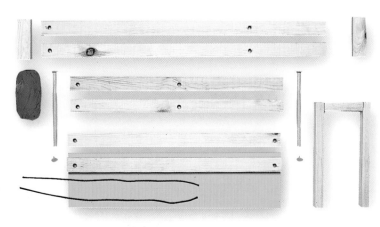

### MAKE it WORK!
This simple drawbridge operates using a counterbalance. The weight of the **deck** is balanced by the weight on the **lever arm**.

**You will need**
pieces of dowel
strips of wood
stiff cardboard
modeling clay
thumbtacks
a glue gun
string
a drill

**1** Cut the wood to length as shown. You will need two pieces about 8 in. long, four pieces 6 in. long and two pieces 2 in. long. Drill holes at the positions indicated.

**2** To make the deck, cut a piece of cardboard measuring 2 in. x 6 in. Glue two of the 6-in. strips of wood along its edges.

**3** Cut a piece of dowel into two rods about 3½ in. long. Make two 2-in. cardboard sleeves for the rods. Line up the holes in one end of the deck with those midway along the two remaining 6-in. strips. Slide a dowel rod through the holes and push thumbtacks into the ends of the rod to keep it in place.

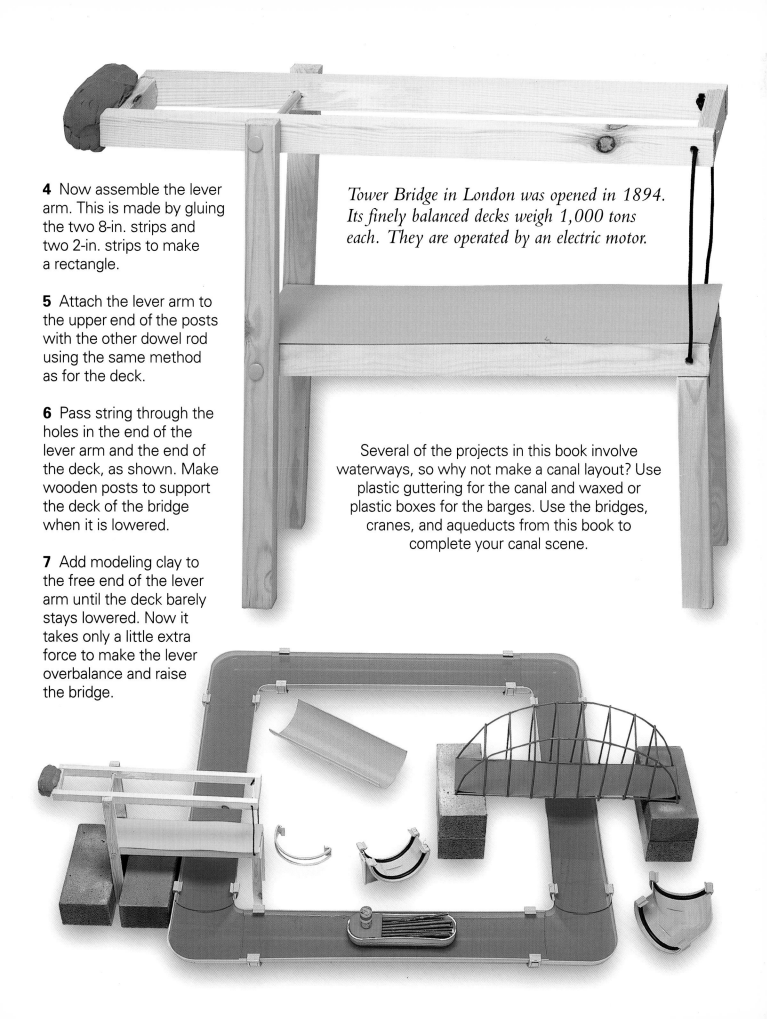

**4** Now assemble the lever arm. This is made by gluing the two 8-in. strips and two 2-in. strips to make a rectangle.

**5** Attach the lever arm to the upper end of the posts with the other dowel rod using the same method as for the deck.

**6** Pass string through the holes in the end of the lever arm and the end of the deck, as shown. Make wooden posts to support the deck of the bridge when it is lowered.

**7** Add modeling clay to the free end of the lever arm until the deck barely stays lowered. Now it takes only a little extra force to make the lever overbalance and raise the bridge.

*Tower Bridge in London was opened in 1894. Its finely balanced decks weigh 1,000 tons each. They are operated by an electric motor.*

Several of the projects in this book involve waterways, so why not make a canal layout? Use plastic guttering for the canal and waxed or plastic boxes for the barges. Use the bridges, cranes, and aqueducts from this book to complete your canal scene.

How can a bridge made from blocks or bricks hold together without glue or cement? A flat brick bridge would fall apart under its own weight alone. However, by arranging the blocks in an arch you can produce a structure of great strength that holds itself in place.

## MAKE it WORK!

To build an arch you will need blocks that have sloping ends that fit together to make a curve. Wooden crates would be best to use, but you could make your own blocks from cardboard.

## You will need

crates with sloping sides
two friends to
    help you
bricks

**1** Try to judge how long your bridge will be. Place two piles of bricks this distance apart on the floor to keep the ends of the arch from sliding apart. Move them in or out if the sides of the arch will not meet.

**2** With a friend, start fitting the crates together, working in from both ends at once. You will need to hold the crates in place as you build. (This may take some practice.)

## Note

Make sure the crates you haven't used yet are within easy reach!

**3** Ask another friend to add the **keystone** to complete the arch. The heavier the load on top of the arch, the more the boxes press on the keystone. This is how the arch stays up without glue or other fasteners.

▲ The first ever bridge was probably made from a straight tree trunk laid across a stream. You can make a simple straight bridge with a plank and two plastic buckets. Can you feel the bridge bending when you stand in the middle?

*An arch can span a much wider gap and carry a much heavier load than a straight bridge. The first arched bridges were made of stone. Today, builders use concrete or wood for arch bridges that have a short span. Arch bridges with long spans are built of concrete or steel.*

Cars and trains on bridges are familiar sights, but a boat crossing a bridge is more of a surprise. Yet this is just what happens with an aqueduct. The strong arches that support an aqueduct carry a canal full of water above the ground.

## You will need

plastic guttering with end caps
a sharp knife        stiff cardboard
a metal ruler         a baseboard
bricks                        glue

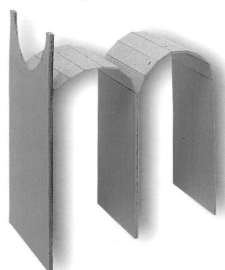

**1** The arches of this aqueduct are each made from a strip of stiff cardboard that measures about 4 in. x 13 3/4 in. Cut the strips to size with the ruler and sharp knife. Be careful with the knife.

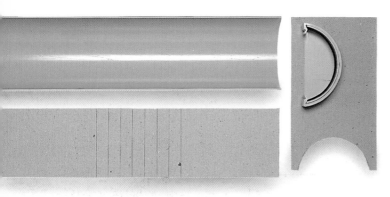

### MAKE it WORK!

Use a row of cardboard arches to support the weight of a plastic canal in your own aqueduct.

**2 Score** eight lines 3/4 in. apart across the middle of a strip of cardboard. Bend the strip to make a shallow arch with two supports.

**3** Take another strip of cardboard, and on it draw a semicircle, using the end of the gutter as a guide. Cut along the line to leave a curve in which the guttering can rest.

**4** Glue together a pair of arches and a gutter support. Your aqueduct is assembled from three or four of these basic units.

*The ancient Romans were skilled engineers. They built aqueducts to supply their cities with water. A famous Roman aqueduct, the Pont du Gard, still stands across a river in France.*

**5** Put the aqueduct together on a baseboard. If necessary, support the walls at either end with bricks.

The arches of your aqueduct support the weight of the canal evenly along its length. But what is the best design for the arches? Should they be flat or very pointed? Experiment with different shapes of arches to see which is the strongest and which is most stable.

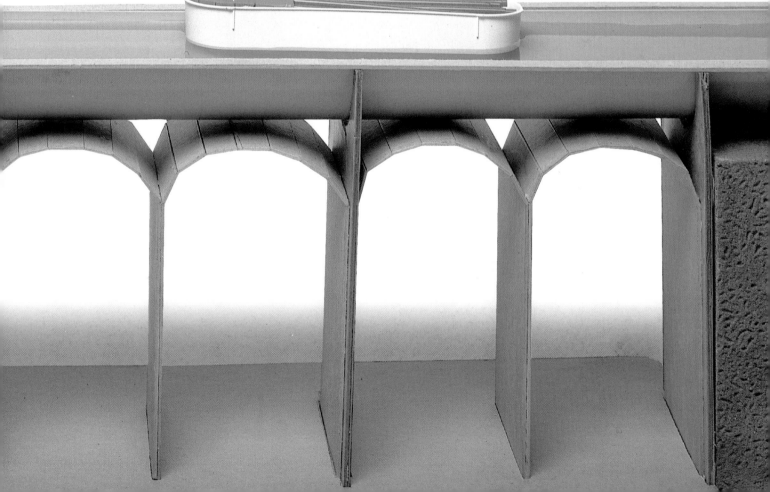

Stone and brick are strong, but they are very heavy. For a long bridge, which has to support its own weight as well as the loads that cross it, lighter materials are needed. Engineers use steel girders, linked together in **lattice** patterns, to build long bridges that are strong, light, and not too expensive.

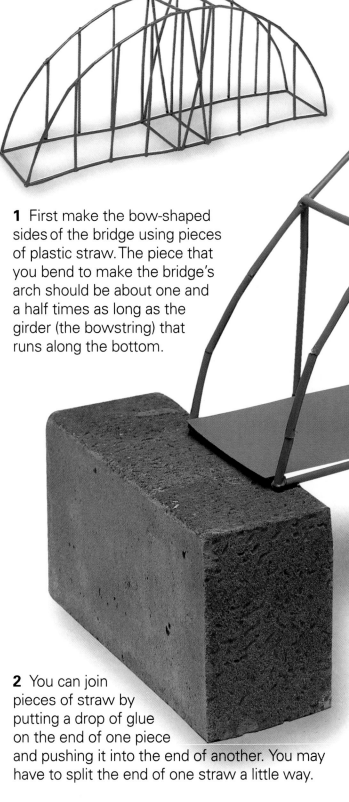

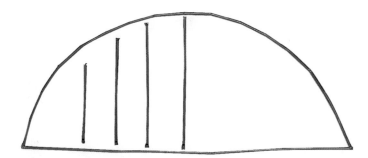

## MAKE it WORK!

Bowstring bridges are named after the string of an archer's bow. Tension in the bridge's bottom girder—the bowstring—holds the arch in place, just as tension in the string curves a bow. Find out how the **ties** carry the strength of the arch to the deck by building your own bridge.

**1** First make the bow-shaped sides of the bridge using pieces of plastic straw. The piece that you bend to make the bridge's arch should be about one and a half times as long as the girder (the bowstring) that runs along the bottom.

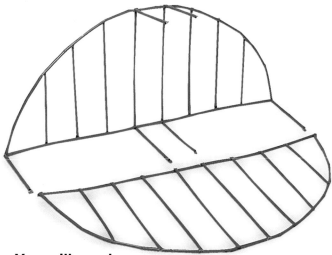

## You will need

bricks
scissors
plastic straws     glue
                thin cardboard

**2** You can join pieces of straw by putting a drop of glue on the end of one piece and pushing it into the end of another. You may have to split the end of one straw a little way.

**3** To attach the ends of the bowstring girder to the arch, split the ends of the bowstring straws. Open out the ends to make small flaps, then cut one of the flaps off each end. Glue the remaining flaps to the ends of the arch. Use this method to attach the ties between the arch and bowstring.

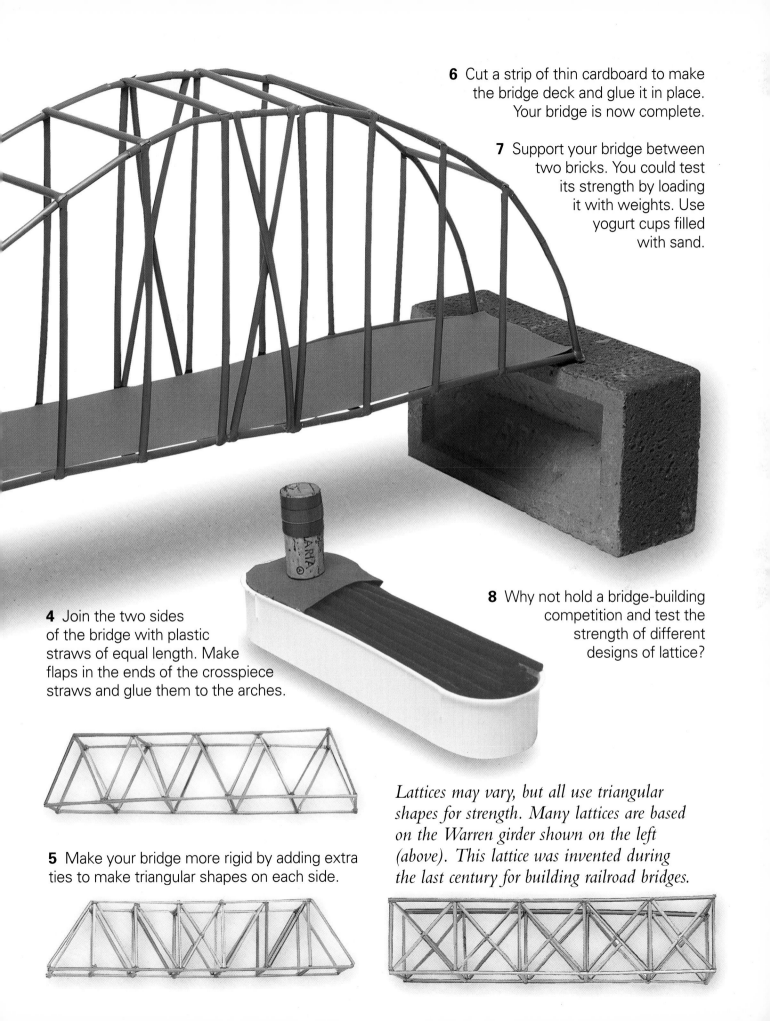

**6** Cut a strip of thin cardboard to make the bridge deck and glue it in place. Your bridge is now complete.

**7** Support your bridge between two bricks. You could test its strength by loading it with weights. Use yogurt cups filled with sand.

**4** Join the two sides of the bridge with plastic straws of equal length. Make flaps in the ends of the crosspiece straws and glue them to the arches.

**8** Why not hold a bridge-building competition and test the strength of different designs of lattice?

**5** Make your bridge more rigid by adding extra ties to make triangular shapes on each side.

*Lattices may vary, but all use triangular shapes for strength. Many lattices are based on the Warren girder shown on the left (above). This lattice was invented during the last century for building railroad bridges.*

A good way to cross a river is on a rope tied between two trees. This simple idea is used to build the world's longest, most elegant bridges. The weight of the traffic crossing a suspension bridge is carried by the two massive cables strung between the towers of the bridge.

## You will need

| | |
|---|---|
| six bricks | strips of cardboard |
| wire staples | nylon string |
| strips of wood | glue |
| awl or leather punch | |

**1** Cut four 8-in. wooden strips and four 2½-in. strips. Glue them together to make the towers, as shown.

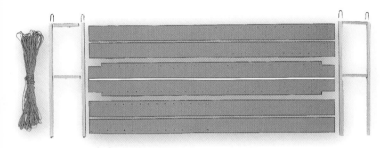

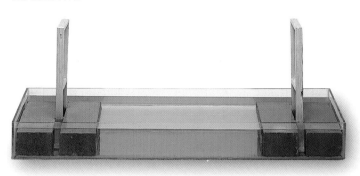

### MAKE it WORK!

The cables in a real suspension bridge must carry thousands of tons of weight. They are wound from strong steel wires and can be over 3 feet thick.

The cables in this model are made from nylon string, but the same principle is at work.

**2** Stand the towers about 16 in. apart using four bricks to keep them in place.

**3** Cut three strips of cardboard measuring 16 in. x 2½ in. to make the main deck and the two approach ramps, as shown.

**4** Punch small holes every ¾ in. along both edges of the cardboard strips. Use an awl or better still, if you have one, a leather punch.

**5** For the bridge cables, stretch two long pieces of string over the towers, attaching them to the tops of the towers with staples. Place the spare bricks on either side of the bridge and tie the ends of the strings around them.

**7** Finally, tie pieces of string every ¾ in. along the cables of the bridge, as shown. Pass them through the holes in the deck of the bridge and knot them tightly underneath. For extra strength, adjust the lengths of string to make the deck flex into an arch.

You could use your bridge and a water tank to make a river crossing like the one below.

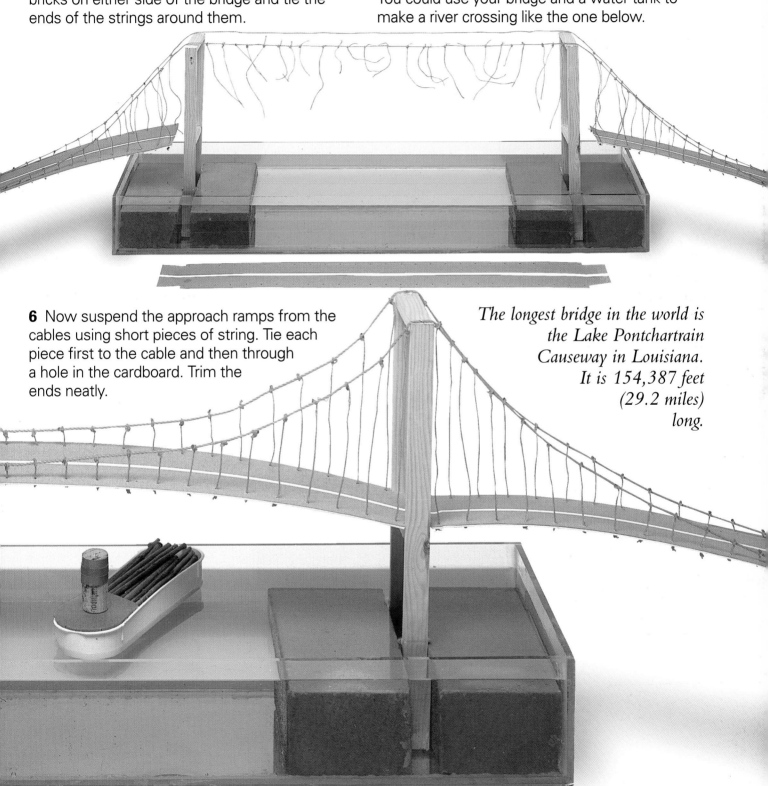

**6** Now suspend the approach ramps from the cables using short pieces of string. Tie each piece first to the cable and then through a hole in the cardboard. Trim the ends neatly.

*The longest bridge in the world is the Lake Pontchartrain Causeway in Louisiana. It is 154,387 feet (29.2 miles) long.*

Making a strong waterproof roof can be the most difficult part of building a house. Flat roofs often leak. A sloping roof works better because the water runs off, but the roof must be strong enough to support the weight of heavy tiles and to stand up to high winds.

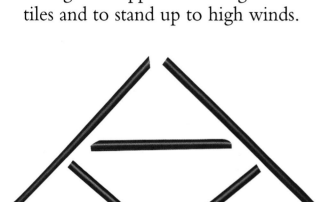

**MAKE it WORK!**

The roof of a modern house is made from a framework of triangles called **trusses**. The sloping sides of each truss are called **rafters**. The rafters are linked across the bottom by a **tie beam**. A series of trusses can be linked together to build a roof of any length.

**You will need**
cardboard
a glue gun                 a knife
thin dowels               plastic straws

**1** Cut six pieces of straw with angled ends as shown. Glue the three longer pieces together into a triangular truss. Glue the three shorter pieces inside, as shown below, to give the truss extra strength.

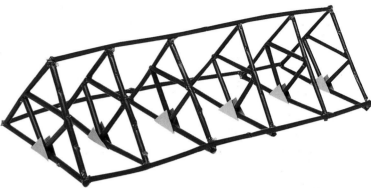

**2** Reinforce the joints at the base of the truss with small cardboard gussets.

**3** Make five more identical trusses. To join them together in a roof frame, glue the trusses to three long straws by their points. Make the trusses an equal distance apart.

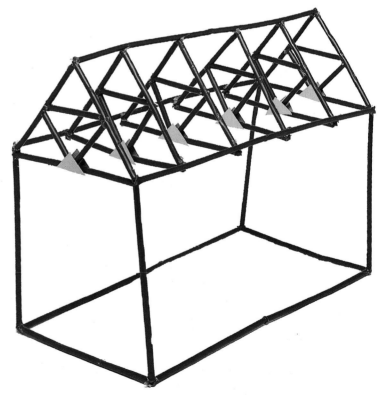

**4** Use more straws to build the framework of a house to support your roof.

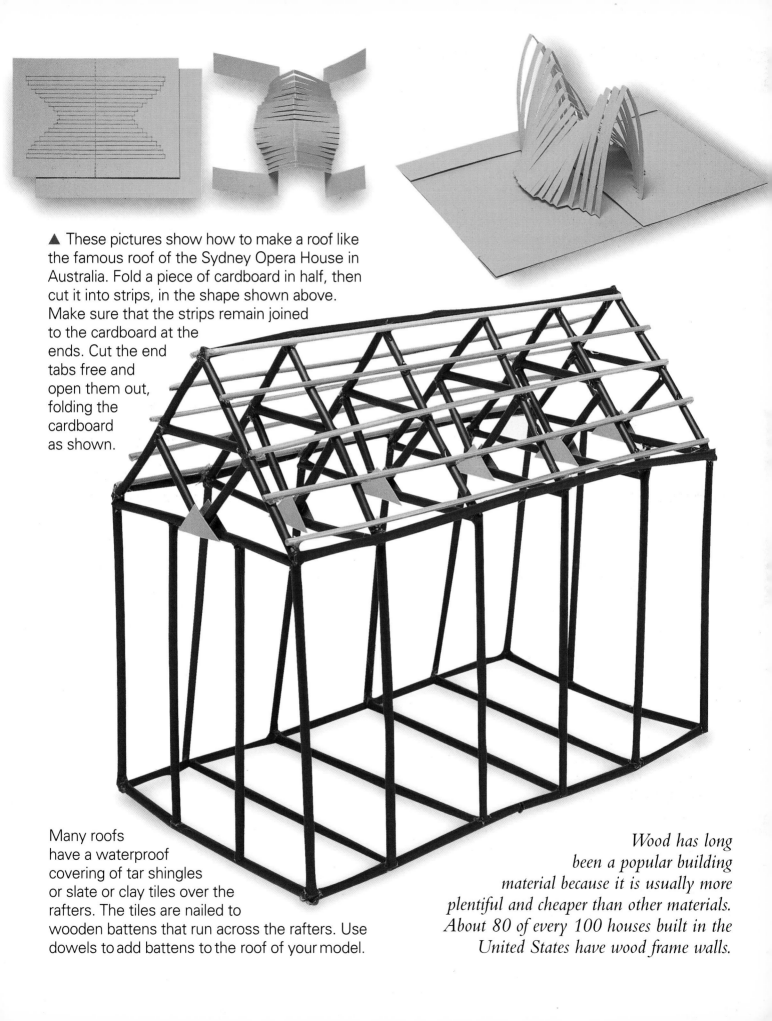

▲ These pictures show how to make a roof like the famous roof of the Sydney Opera House in Australia. Fold a piece of cardboard in half, then cut it into strips, in the shape shown above. Make sure that the strips remain joined to the cardboard at the ends. Cut the end tabs free and open them out, folding the cardboard as shown.

Many roofs have a waterproof covering of tar shingles or slate or clay tiles over the rafters. The tiles are nailed to wooden battens that run across the rafters. Use dowels to add battens to the roof of your model.

*Wood has long been a popular building material because it is usually more plentiful and cheaper than other materials. About 80 of every 100 houses built in the United States have wood frame walls.*

Stone Age people built their homes out of the natural materials around them. Using only a flint knife, they cut sticks, tied them into a frame with dry grass, and then covered the frame with a skin to make a tent.

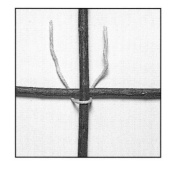 

Some sticks will need to be tied so that they cross. The pictures above show you how to do this using a short piece of string. Some sticks must be tied lengthwise. The picture along the bottom of the page shows you how to overlap the sticks and tie them with two knots.

## MAKE it WORK!

Make your own Stone Age tent with flexible sticks tied into a dome-shaped lattice.

## You will need

long flexible sticks (plant stakes from a gardening supply store are ideal)
safety goggles
scissors
string

**1** Start by making a ring of sticks for the base of the tent. Tie sticks together as shown below, bending them as you go.

**2** When you have a complete ring, lay it on the ground. Wearing the goggles, take long sticks, or short ones tied together, and make hoops at intervals across the ring. Tie the ring about 4 in. from the ends of the hoops. The hoops should meet above the middle of the ring.

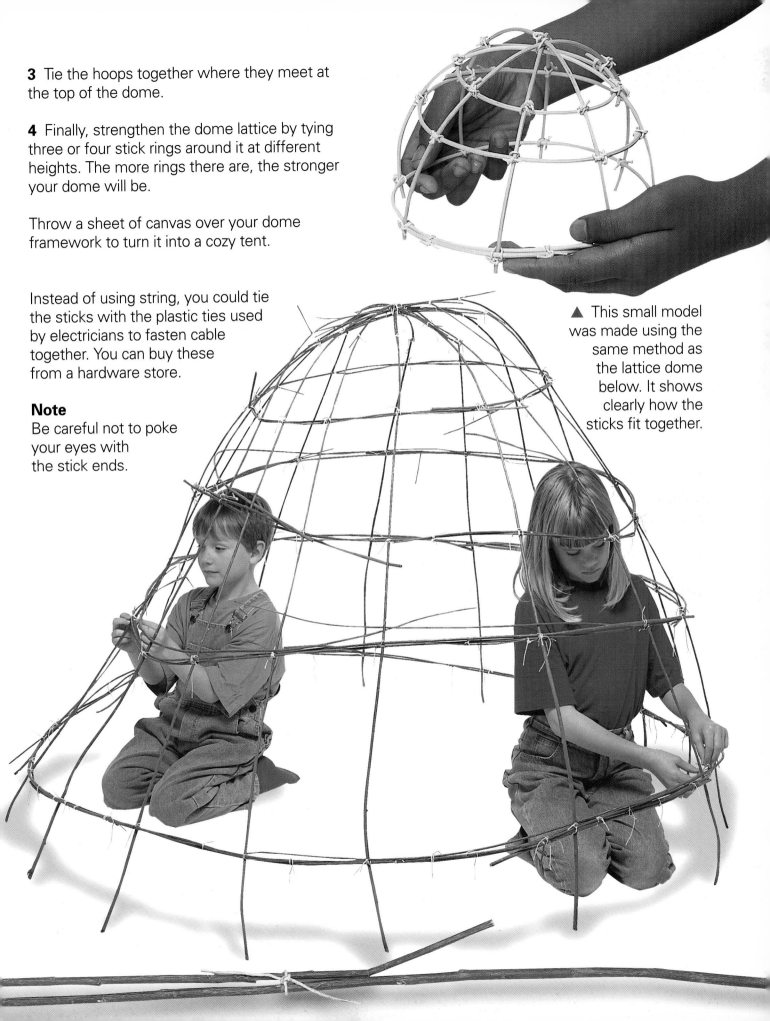

**3** Tie the hoops together where they meet at the top of the dome.

**4** Finally, strengthen the dome lattice by tying three or four stick rings around it at different heights. The more rings there are, the stronger your dome will be.

Throw a sheet of canvas over your dome framework to turn it into a cozy tent.

Instead of using string, you could tie the sticks with the plastic ties used by electricians to fasten cable together. You can buy these from a hardware store.

**Note**
Be careful not to poke your eyes with the stick ends.

▲ This small model was made using the same method as the lattice dome below. It shows clearly how the sticks fit together.

Cardboard boxes are made by folding flat sheets of cardboard and gluing the edges together. But what shape should the cardboard sheet be in order to make a cube-shaped box? Try taking a box apart to find out. The flat sheet that this box was built from is made up of six squares joined at the edges.

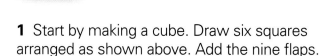

## MAKE it WORK!

The flat starting shape used to make a box is called a **net**. The solid shape it makes when it is folded is called a **form**. The examples on this page show how different nets fold up to make different solid forms. Try making some of them yourself.

## You will need

a pair of drawing compasses
a pair of scissors
thin cardboard
a pencil
a ruler
glue

**1** Start by making a cube. Draw six squares arranged as shown above. Add the nine flaps.

**2** Cut out the cube net and its glue flaps.

**3** Fold the net along the dotted lines and glue the flaps inside the edges of the squares where they meet.

When you have completed the cube, try to make some more difficult shapes.

A pyramid made from four equal-sided triangles (see far left) is called a tetrahedron. The blue pyramid with the square base is the same shape as the pyramids of Egypt.

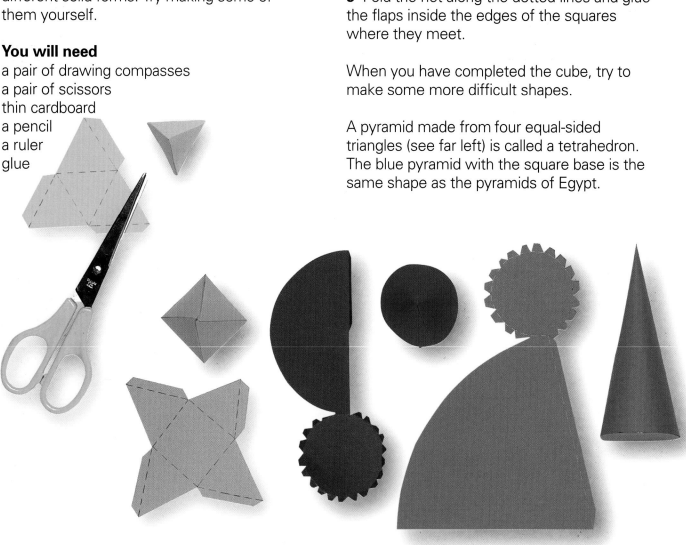

To make cones, use your compasses to draw circles joined to semi-circles, as shown. Experiment to see how changing the radius of each curve affects the cone's shape.

▼ The long nets below fold into shapes called prisms. The three-sided shape is a triangular prism and the six-sided one is a hexagonal prism.

▲ The six-pointed net above folds to make a six-sided pyramid. The four-pointed star folds into a tall shape like an Egyptian **obelisk**.

Make a mobile out of some of your shapes by hanging them from pieces of thread attached to dowels. You could even make your own gift boxes.

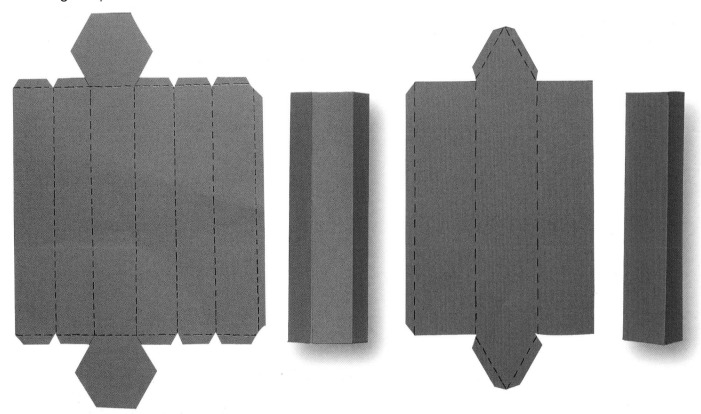

Try peeling an orange, keeping the skin in one piece. Flatten out the peel onto a board. What does it look like? The skin tears into several parts with curved edges, which are joined together. The shapes below are like the flattened-out orange peel. They are called polyhedrons, from the Greek word meaning "objects with many sides."

## MAKE it WORK!
The nets below are like the flattened orange skin. They fold up into shapes with so many sides that they are almost spheres.

### You will need
| | |
|---|---|
| cardboard | a protractor |
| a ruler | scissors |
| glue | a pencil |

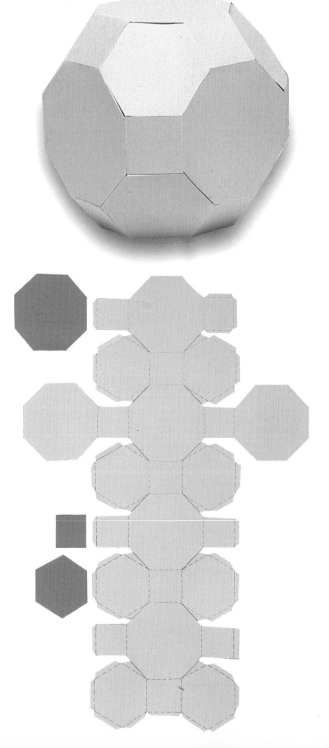

**1** Make cardboard templates for the basic shapes that make up each net, shown in red cardboard below. (You can use a protractor for this or trace the red shapes and enlarge them.)

**2** Draw around your templates to make the net for your polyhedron.

**3** Add the glue flaps to your net. Finally, fold up the net along the dotted lines and glue the flaps in place. This may take some patience!

*The third polyhedron from the left is made from pentagons and hexagons. This pattern is often used to make soccer balls.*

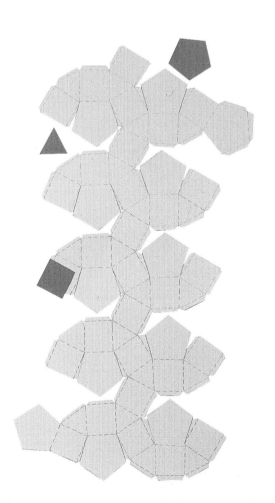

An Inuit's igloo is made from blocks of ice fitted together to make a dome. Domes are strong and hold heat well because their surface is small compared with the space inside. The designer Buckminster Fuller saw that large domes could be made by joining together simple flat shapes.

## MAKE it WORK!
The igloo on this page is made entirely out of two simple shapes—triangles and pentagons —joined together.

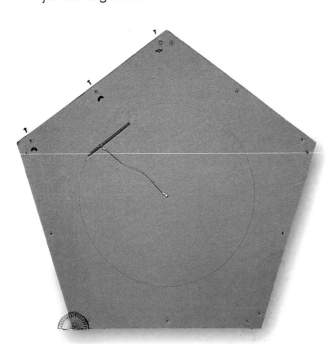

## You will need

| | |
|---|---|
| an awl | a screwdriver |
| a pencil | a sharp knife |
| wing nuts and screws | a steel ruler |
| large sheets of strong cardboard | |
| an adult and friends to help you | |

**1** With an adult, measure and cut out the shapes below. The sides of each shape should measure 2 ft. You will need ten triangles with flaps on each side, and six pentagons. Put one pentagon aside to be the roof.

**2** Cut a large hole in one of the remaining pentagons to make a door.

**3** Join a triangle to one side of each of the five remaining pentagons. Fasten the pieces together with screws and wing nuts. Use the awl to make holes for the screws. (You could use hook-and-loop fastener patches instead of screws to join the shapes together.)

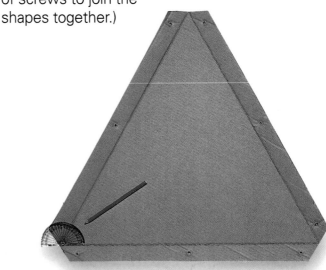

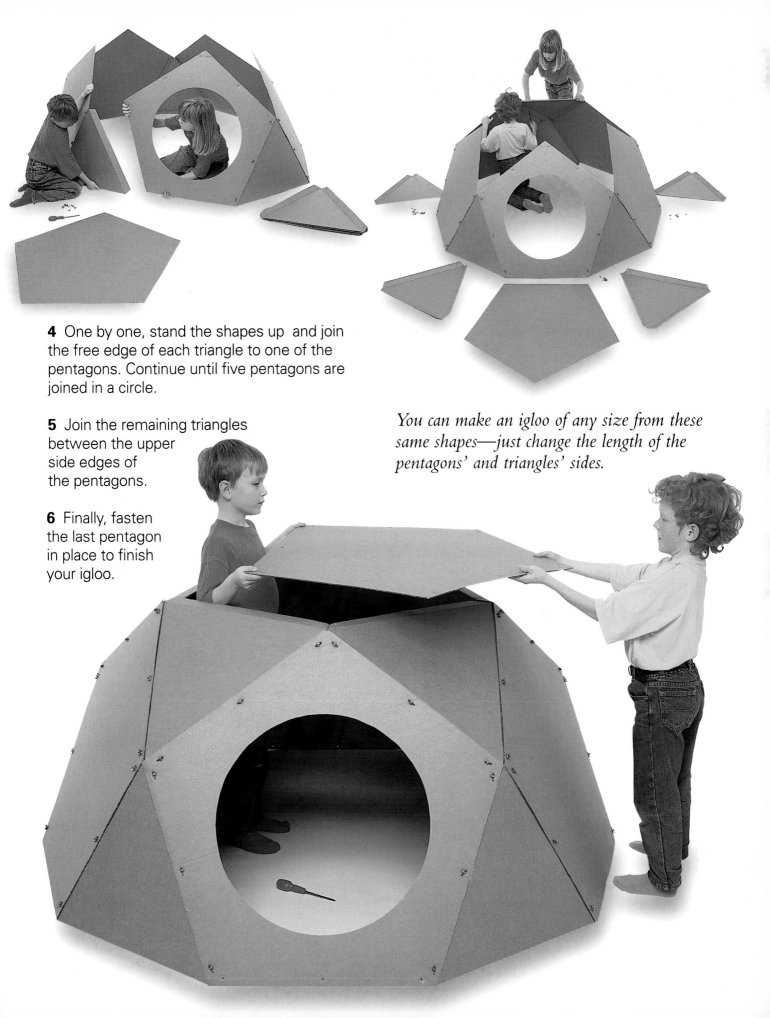

**4** One by one, stand the shapes up and join the free edge of each triangle to one of the pentagons. Continue until five pentagons are joined in a circle.

**5** Join the remaining triangles between the upper side edges of the pentagons.

**6** Finally, fasten the last pentagon in place to finish your igloo.

*You can make an igloo of any size from these same shapes—just change the length of the pentagons' and triangles' sides.*

Building in outer space is difficult. Astronauts have to wear clumsy spacesuits, and all the things they use must be transported from Earth by rocket. It takes a lot of fuel to carry heavy materials into space. **Modules** made up of simple shapes weigh less and are easy to build.

## You will need

| | |
|---|---|
| a sharp knife | a pencil |
| thick cardboard | a ruler |
| a friend to help | |

screws and wing nuts or hook-and-loop
  fastener patches

**1** Cut out and assemble the parts of an igloo as described on pages 176-177.

**2** Build a second igloo.

## MAKE it WORK!

The igloo on page 177 is made from just two simple shapes. By joining two igloos together, you can make yourself a space module. You could then link several modules together with short tunnels to build yourself a space station. The different modules could be used for eating, sleeping, and working.

**3** Turn one of the igloos upside down.

**4** Lift the second igloo and place it on top of the first. Line up the pentagons of the top half with the triangles of the bottom half.

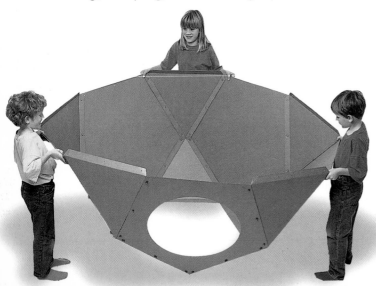

**5** Fasten the two igloos together with wing nuts and screws or hook-and-loop fastener patches.

Your space module is now complete.

*A space station is a place where people can live and work in space. Larger space stations are made using modules. Rockets or space shuttles carry modules of the station into space, where astronauts assemble them.*

**Acid**   A word used by pharmacists to describe one of two kinds of chemical substances. Acidic foods, such as lemons, taste sour or sharp. Strong acids are dangerous and can burn holes in wood or cloth.

**Alkaline**   A word used by pharmacists to describe one of two kinds of chemical substances. In chemistry, an alkali is the opposite of an acid. Mixing things with acids and alkalis often causes chemical reactions, such as in a battery. Alkaline batteries are often used for bicycle lights, walkie-talkies, and other electrical toys.

**Amplify**   When you amplify something, you make it louder.

**Antenna**   A long piece of wire or metal that picks up radio waves. All radios and televisions need an antenna.

**Arched**   Built in a curve. When a force such as the weight of traffic or water presses on an arch, the blocks of the arch are pressed together and held more firmly in place.

**Atomic power**   Energy that comes from making changes to the center of an atom. By splitting atoms, an enormous amount of heat is created. This heat is used to boil water, making steam to drive turbines and produce electricity.

**Atoms**   Tiny particles, more than a million times smaller than the thickness of a human hair. Everything around us is made up of atoms – they are like building blocks, and by combining different atoms in different ways, different substances are created.

**Axle**   A rod or shaft around which wheels and gears turn.

**Ball bearings**   Ball bearings help to reduce friction when a wheel turns around an axle. The steel balls are placed so that they roll between the wheel and the axle.

**Boom**   A long pole or girder used to position loads, which can swing on a hinge at one end of the pole. A boom is used for a yacht's sail as well as the load on a crane.

**Bridge**   In a string instrument, the bridge is a small, raised piece of wood or metal that connects the strings to the soundboard.

**Cam**   An oval shaped wheel, or a wheel whose axle does not go through the center. It is used to change a turning movement into an up-and-down movement.

**Circuit**   A loop-shaped path along which electricity can flow.

**Cochlea**   A curly tube inside the ear, filled with liquid and lined with tiny hairs. The cochlea turns the vibrations that sound waves make against the eardrum into nerve pulses.

**Commutator**   A special kind of electrical connection, used in electric motors. A commutator makes the direction of the electric current change at regular intervals.

**Component**   In electronics, a component is one single part of a whole circuit. For example, a switch or a battery is a component in an electrical circuit.

**Compressed**   If something is compressed, it is squashed or squeezed together by force. Compressed air stores energy that can be used to propel a model rocket. The force of compression squashes a cushion when you sit on it. The bricks at the base of a tall tower are compressed by the weight of the bricks above them pushing down.

**Conductor**   In electronics, a conductor is any substance that an electric current can pass through.

**Counterbalance**   A weight used to balance the load being lifted by a lever arm.

**Current electricity**   Current electricity is the electricity we use in homes, offices, and factories. It is produced in power stations and is then distributed through wires, pylons, and transformers.

**Decibel**   A decibel is the unit for measuring how loud or soft a sound is.

**Deck**   The floor or platform of a bridge, over which traffic passes.

**Diode**   A tube-shaped device used in electronic circuits. The diode stops the current flowing both ways through the circuit, making it flow in one direction.

**Drive belt**   A loop of rubber or other material that carries power from one pulley to another.

**Drive chain**   A loop of chain that does the same job as a drive belt. The links of the chain fit around the teeth on gears called sprockets. A bicycle chain is an example of a drive chain.

**Eardrum**   The part of the ear inside the head that vibrates when struck by sound waves.

**Efficient**   An efficient machine does its job without wasting energy. Oil, for instance, helps many machines to run smoothly and efficiently by reducing the amount of friction that occurs between moving parts.

**Effort**   The force (a push or a pull) needed to work a lever or a pulley.

**Electrolyte**   A liquid solution that is able to conduct electricity. Batteries use electrolytes to make electricity.

**Electromagnets**   When an electric current passes through a metal, such as a piece of iron or copper, it always produces a magnetic field. Electromagnets are useful because their magnetism can be switched on and off with the electric current.

**Electrons**   Tiny particles of atoms. Each electron carries an electrical charge.

**Electroscope**   A scientific instrument used to measure the strength of an electrical charge.

**Energy**   Energy is needed to do any kind of job or action. Motors and engines use energy, and so do our bodies. The energy stored in fuels such as gasoline is used to power engines. People use the energy stored in their muscles for all physical activities. The food we eat, and the electricity that powers an electric motor, are both called energy sources.

**Engine**   A machine that uses the energy from a fuel, such as coal or gasoline, to do work like lifting loads or turning wheels.

**Engineers**   Engineers use scientific knowledge to invent and make things. Besides machines, they design roads, bridges, and buildings.

**Experiments**   Special methods and procedures designed to test hypotheses (*see separate entry*) about how the world works.

**Filament**   A thin coil of wire, usually made from the element tungsten, inside a light bulb. The electricity has to work so hard to push its way through the tungsten that the coil glows and gives off light.

**Force**   A push or a pull, used to lift something, start it moving, or hold it in place against another force such as gravity. Forces on a building either squeeze, stretch, or twist its parts. If the structure of the building is not strong enough, the parts may snap or buckle.

**Force field**   The area around a source of energy (such as a magnet) where the energy works.

**Form**   A shape, for example one that is created by folding up a paper net (*see separate entry*).

**Fossil fuels**   Coal, oil, and natural gas are fossil fuels. They are formed from the remains of ancient plants and animals that have been buried for thousands of years beneath layers of mud and rock.

**Foundation**   The part of a building that is hidden beneath the ground. The foundations of a building spread its weight over a larger area and reduce the pressure on its base.

**Friction**   A dragging force that stops things sliding across each other smoothly. There is more friction produced by rough surfaces, such as sandpaper, than by smooth surfaces, like ice. Friction produces heat (like when you rub your hands together to keep warm) and makes two objects stick together (like tires gripping the road).

**Fulcrum**   The hinge or pivot around which a lever turns.

**Gears**   Toothed wheels that link together and carry turning movement from one place to another. Gears are also used to change the speed and direction of movement.

**Generator**   A machine that turns heat or movement into an electrical current.

**Girders**   Beams made from iron or steel.

**Gondolas**   The cabins in which the passengers travel on a cable car.

**Graphite**   The substance that pencil leads are made out of. Pencils contained lead until it was discovered that graphite was a better writing material.

**Gravity**   The force that makes objects fall toward the Earth and makes them feel heavy.

**Guy ropes**   Ropes used to steady the poles and canvas of a tent.

**Gyrocompass**   An instrument that always points in the same direction because it contains a spinning gyroscope.

**Headers**   Bricks laid at right angles to the face of a wall.

**Hertz**   Sound waves are measured in a unit called the Hertz. It is named after the German physicist, Heinrich Hertz.

**Hub**   The center of a wheel. The axle usually goes through the hub.

**Hydroelectric power/hydroelectricity**
Electricity produced by the energy of water flowing through a generator.

**Hydroelectric turbine**   A machine turned by flowing water, which is connected to an electricity generator.

**Hypothesis**   A scientific guess based on known facts.

**Incus**   One of the three main bones inside the ear. Often also called the anvil bone.

**Insulation**   Foam or other materials that keep heat from escaping from a building.

**Insulators**   Materials that do not conduct electricity. Rubber and plastic are both good insulators.

**Keystone**   The topmost stone of an arch, which holds the rest in place.

**Lattice**   A structure made by joining rods or beams into regular patterns. Lattices made from triangles are usually chosen for building, because triangular shapes are strong.

**Lever**   A rod or bar that rests on a pivot. A load at one end of the lever can be lifted by applying an effort at the other end.

**Lever arm**   A hinged arm that is used to lift heavy loads.

**Load**   The weight or force that is moved by applying effort to a lever or pulley. The part of an electric circuit that uses the electric power is also called a load. In a lighting circuit, the load is the light bulb.

**Magnetism**   A natural, invisible force that makes certain metals attract or repel one another.

**Malleus**   One of the bones inside the ear. It is also called the hammer bone.

**Materials**   Substances, such as plastics, that are used to make other objects.

**Matter**   All the different substances in the Universe are 'matter'. There are three forms: solids, liquids, and gases.

**Modules**   Simple parts, often made up of regular shapes, that are joined together to build a complicated structure.

**Molecule**   A tiny particle of a substance. Every molecule is made up of two or more atoms joined together.

**Mesh**   The teeth on two gears are meshed when they fit together. One gear turns and its teeth mesh with the teeth on the second gear and make it turn too.

**Musical notation**   Recording music by writing it down on paper.

**Musical score**   A written record of a piece of music.

**Nerve pulses**   Nerve pulses are signals sent out by our organs of sense, such as our eyes and ears. These signals pass along our nerves, to the brain, where they are decoded as sights, sounds, tastes, smells or feelings.

**Net**   A flat sheet, made up of simple shapes joined together, that can be folded up into a solid shape or form.

**Note**  In music, a note is a sound played at a particular pitch.

**Obelisk**  A tall, pointed block of stone. In Egypt, obelisks were carved with prayers and names.

**Octave**  An octave is a scale of eight notes that rise and fall step by step. Most Western music is based on the octave scale.

**Pendulum**  A hanging weight, which swings back and forth because of the force of gravity.

**Percussion instruments**  Musical instruments that are played by being struck or shaken. Drums, maracas, and xylophones are examples of percussion instruments.

**Phonograph**  An early kind of record player. It recorded sounds by making a series of bumps and dips in grooves on a rotating cylinder.

**Physics**  The branch of science that finds out about different kinds of energy and matter. Sound is one of the forms of energy investigated by physicists.

**Pitch**  The pitch of a note is how high or how low it is. If sound waves are close together they make a higher pitch than if they are far apart.

**Pivot**  A hinge or balance point, around which something turns.

**Pneumatic**  Pneumatic machines are driven by compressed air.

**Pole**  One of two points on a magnet where the magnetic force is at its strongest. Like poles repel, and opposite poles attract.

**Pollution**  Waste or garbage which damages the natural world around us.

**Pressure**  The pushing force that acts on an object when it is surrounded by air or water. You can feel the pressure on your ears when you swim underwater. The deeper the water, the greater the pressure.

**Projectile**  A missile thrown by a catapult or fired from a cannon.

**Pulley**  A wheel turned by a rope or drive belt. It changes the direction of a force, or carries it from one place to another.

**Pulley blocks**  Two or more pulleys joined together to lift a large load with a small effort.

**Radio waves**  Waves of electro-magnetic energy that travel rapidly across long distances. Sounds are turned into radio waves by a radio transmitter, and changed back into sound again by a radio receiver.

**Rafters**   The sloping beams that form the frame of a roof.

**Range**   The distance traveled by a projectile between being fired and landing.

**Resistor**   A substance that offers resistance to an electric current.

**Resonator**   A space inside an instrument filled with air, which vibrates and makes the sound of the instrument louder.

**Rotate**   To turn around, like a wheel on an axle.

**Scale**   A series or sequence of different musical notes.

**Score**   To make cuts or lines in an object, so that it will bend more easily. Score lines can be made using the blade of a pair of scissors or a knife and a metal ruler. A **musical score** is a written record of a piece of music.

**Silicon chip**   A tiny, wafer-thin slice of the substance silicon, that has an entire electronic circuit on it, in miniature. Silicon chips are an especially important part of modern computers.

**Sound waves**   Sounds travel through the air in waves. When someone bangs on a drum, for example, the drumhead squashes together the air beside it every time it vibrates. If we could see air, the movement of sound waves would look something like the ripples on a pond when a stone is thrown into the water.

**Soundboard**   The board in a piano or a string instrument which is connected to the strings by the bridge. It vibrates when the strings are struck or plucked.

**Sprockets**   Toothed wheels, usually connected by a drive chain (*see separate entry*).

**Stapes**   One of the bones of the inner ear. It is often also called the stirrup bone.

**Static electricity**   Static electricity is an electrical charge which is produced naturally when two things rub together. Lightning is the best-known example of static electricity.

**Stave**   In music, a stave is a set of five lines on which musical notes are written.

**Stethoscope**   An instrument used by doctors that allows them to listen to the inside of a patient's body.

**String instruments**   String instruments are played by plucking strings or scraping them with a bow. A sitar, a zither, a violin, and a guitar are all examples of string instruments.

**Tension**  A stretching force.

**Terminals**  The points in an electrical circuit where the electric current leaves or enters the circuit.

**Tie beam**  A beam that holds together the ends of two rafters in a roof frame.

**Ties**  Strings or rods that prevent two parts of a structure from separating.

**Trajectory**  The curved path that a projectile follows as it travels through the air.

**Trusses**  Frameworks used to support a roof frame. Trusses are often arranged in triangles.

**Vacuum**  A completely empty space, that does not even contain air. Outer space is a vacuum.

**Vibrate**  When something vibrates, it moves back and forth a small amount very quickly. A guitar string vibrates if you pluck it.

**Volt**  A unit that measures how much power is produced by a source of electricity.

**Watt**  A unit that measures electrical power at the point where it is used in a circuit.

**Winch**  A machine that lifts a load by winding up a rope or chain attached to the load.

**Wind instruments**  Instruments that are played by blowing through them. Trumpets and recorders are both wind instruments.